Cornhole
Throwing Bags in a Hole

MARK ROGERS

amalgam

Copyright © 2011 by Mark Rogers. All Rights Reserved.

Published by Amalgam Studio LLC, Chicago

No Part of this publication may be reproduced, stored in a retrieval system, or transmitted in any form or any means, electronic, mechanical, photocopying, recording, scanning, or otherwise, except as permitted under Section 107 or 108 of the 1976 United States Copyright Act, without either the prior written permission of the Publisher or the Author. Requests to the Publisher for permission should be addressed online http://www.amalgamstudio.com/permissions.

Limit of Liability/ Disclaimer of Warranty: While the publisher and author have used their best efforts in preparing this book, they make no representations or warranties with respect to the accuracy or completeness of the contents of this book and specifically disclaim any implied warranties or merchantability or fitness for a particular purpose. No warranty may be created or extended by sales representatives or written sales materials. The advice and strategies contained herein may not be suitable for your situation. You should consult with a professional where appropriate. Neither the publisher nor author shall be liable for any loss of profit or any other commercial damages, including but not limited to special, incidental, consequential, or other damages.

Amalgam Studio publishes its books in physical and electronic formats. Some content that appears in print may not be available in electronic books, and vice versa. For more information about Amalgam Studio products, please visit our website www.amalgamstudio.com.

ISBN-13 978-0-9845688-3-3

Library of Congress Control Number: 2010916935

Printed in the United States of America

1 2 3 4 5 6 7 8 9 10

To Dean, the coolest Rogers I know.

CONTENTS

FOREWORD	4
OPENING COMMENTARY	10
HISTORY	13
SOCIAL IMPACT	26
CORNHOLE RULES & REGULATIONS	39
RUNNING A CORNHOLE TOURNAMENT	64
HOW TO PITCH IN THE HOLE	85
CORNHOLE STRATEGERY	104
HOW TO BUILD A CORNHOLE BOARD	118
BUILDER COMMUNITY	131
CORNHOLE THE SPORT	138
WE ARE THE CHAMPIONS	153
CORNHOLE PLAYER BIOGRAPHIES	168
CORNHOLE: WHAT'S IN A NAME?	175
CORNHOLE LINGO	182
ACKNOWLEDGEMENTS	194
APPENDIX	196
INDEX	198

FOREWORD

MIKE WHITTON
President, American Cornhole Association

I TOSSED MY FIRST GAME OF CORNHOLE at the age of 11 back in the year 1952. The family had gathered at my grandmother's home in Mount Healthy, Ohio, just fifteen miles north of Cincinnati and known as a refuge from the cholera epidemic of 1850; thus the name. Must have been the end of spring, because I could remember listening to the roar of Formula 1 cars on the radio. They were racing in the Indianapolis 500. Troy Ruttman was leading, when four of my uncles unveiled a board with a hole in it. Us kids gathered around and watched as my uncles leaned the board against my grandmother's garage and started pitching bags at the holes. I had never seen anything like it. We waited, as patiently as kids can at that age, to get a crack at throwing the bags. Lucky for us, the wash tub of beer and ice began to run low and so, without fuel, the men faded. My cousins and I wasted no time and seized the opportunity. We threw bags until what seemed to be midnight, before our parents called us in. Three years later my family and I shipped off to California, and I was not to see the game again for over four decades.

Fast forward to the year 2004, and I found myself again in Ohio, this time for a Whitton family reunion. It had been 30 years since the last reunion of Whitton's, so I set about getting all my married kids to go back with me. My nephew, Chris, organized the gathering and mentioned during his invitation that we were going to play Cornhole. I looked forward to reuniting with family, but I also got excited to throw some bags again. Sure enough, my three sons and I arrived to see a set of board and bags and some beer ready for us. I introduced my sons to the game, playing from four in the afternoon to eight the next morning. They immediately took to the game. We only stopped once for one short hiatus to grab some more brew and a couple of White Castle suit cases. My sons had never eaten a slider, so I got to introduce them to another of my childhood loves.

The enjoyment of the game had not waned a bit for me, since the summer of '52. It became clear from that point forward that Cornhole is the perfect bridge between ages, abilities and attitudes. At the close of our reunion pitching, my sons and I sat down for a power breakfast of cold White Castles. We came to the conclusion that Cornhole is the greatest backyard game of all time. I talked further with my sons, about the allure of the game, and how we wanted to take a more active role in facilitating play outside our circle. One point we wanted to address was the structuring of the rules and standards. Depending on whose yard you were in, the rules would vary. We decided to start an association that better defined the structure of the game while maintaining the inherent fun the game allows. We headed back from the reunion in mid-August and by October the ACA's website was operational.

The American Cornhole Association was born, and to date we boast over 30,000 members in 12 countries. We have sanctioned tournaments from the U.S.A. to Australia, Panama, Costa Rica, England, Sweden and Germany. I believe the game of Cornhole is in its budding stage of expansion, and I do not foresee any slowing in the growth and interest of the game.

The ACA mission starts with bringing family and neighbors together to introduce them to the game of Cornhole. This never rung so true than the day the family and I took a trip to Doheny Beach. The beach is comprised of 5 acres of sand and grass, a perfect recreation setting. We needed all that room for my family, in-laws, friends, grand-kids and friends of grand-kids. We set-up shop at a picnic area, displaying our food and drink and of course, our Cornhole sets. We had brought two. After settling, the first bags started flying at one of the sets. The other momentarily sat vacant. Before too long an Asian man approached me. In tow, he too, had a very large family, who were curious about the game we were playing. In broken English, he asked how to play, and I proceeded to teach. I set him up at the vacant board. Explaining in words became a challenge, but showing him through pantomiming did the trick. After a few displays of the bag being tossed and basic rules, his family began enjoying the game. That teacher-student experience spoke volumes to the simplicity of the game and its cross-cultural appeal. In no time another family was hooked. As the afternoon progressed we found that our families had intermixed, playing both Cornhole and sharing each others picnic feasts.

A description I hear quite a bit about the game of Cornhole is that it's quite simply, great fun. Never have I had more fun tossing bags than when I participated in a tournament at a nudist camp. I was invited to a local rock radio station to talk Cornhole with a disc jockey and his audience. The conversation turned risque and I found myself describing a version of Cornhole a couple of Buckeye college students had told me about. The altered version is penned Striphole, where if one does not score, they drink, and if all four bags manage to miss the deck, then the errant thrower must remove an article of clothing. There must be a lot of naked Buckeyes, because it is easy to miss the board if you are a beginner and sober, let alone tipsy. This grabbed the attention of one listener, who called and proclaimed she had a better version of Striphole. She practiced nudism, and asked if I would be interested to hold a Cornhole tournament at her local nudist ranch. I obliged. Being a married man of 52 years, I should tread lightly, but I will say the experience was fun, distracting and humbling all in one. I learned that sagging tattoos make a great argument for laser removal, and a few guys should have been arrested for insufficient exposure. And that a Cornhole bag doesn't cover much. At the end of the day the experience was completely new (or nude) to me and I had a blast playing Cornhole the way nature intended.

ACA members send me news of their unusual experiences. The members of the ACA come from many places with many stories. I recently received correspondence from a group of hikers, one of which trekked with a board strapped to his back. The frame of the deck rose above his head. A picture, he sent, shows him being assisted by two girls, with two other gentlemen trailing behind. Upon reaching an altitude of 14,000 feet, they unloaded their Cornhole gear and played a game. From what I know, this is the highest game of Cornhole played on the record.

I also find myself running into Buckeye fans wherever I go. I have traveled this country of ours from coast to coast numerous times and one thing is clear; Buckeye fans are multiplying to every nook and cranny of the U.S.A. and are bringing the game of Cornhole with them. I work for a large national company and was sent on an excursion for a sales meeting. Usually, meetings like these kick-off with an icebreaker to loosen everybody up. Normally this exercise can be somewhat cheesy, but it gets the job done. When I walked into a large, open meeting room, much to my surprise, a couple decks were laid out before us. Now this was my kind of icebreaker. Turns out our national sales manager is not only an avid Buckeye fan, but loves the game of Cornhole. When I found out he was also a member of the ACA, I pulled rank, letting him know I was the President of the ACA and in turn of this icebreaker.

Another method of the Cornhole word reaching out is through our armed services. I constantly hear from every branch of the military who are serving in Iraq, Afghanistan, Europe, Asia, pretty much everywhere that our brave men and woman are stationed. Our membership is truly worldwide. The letters I receive from our brothers and sisters in the military are the most rewarding for me. I always make sure to send some Cornhole gear to them, whether that be bags, hats, shirts and cozies. Many times our servicemen will send me some pictures of them and their fellow soldiers tossing bags. One snapshot particularly caught my eye; it was a General and a full-bird colonel participating in a tournament they ended up winning.

I hope to bring the game to as many people as possible. I welcome you to the game and know that after playing a few years, you too will have some good stories to tell. Make sure to let your friends and family in on the fun, as we grow our Cornhole community. Just remember the first rule of the game is to have fun.

OPENING COMMENTARY

"All the great things are simple, and many can be expressed in a single word: freedom, justice, honor, duty, mercy, hope."
 -Winston Churchill

So there I was... during the second weekend of existence into my child's life, my wife gave me the green light to forego diapers and bodily gas, in lieu of a road trip with my bud Don. What could tear me away from the cute blob stage of my son's life? Cornhole. That's right, I made a five hour trip from Chicago to the Mecca of Cornhole, Cincinnati, Ohio for the Tailgate Bash World Championships. We stopped along I-65 to fuel up the car and grab some drinks and three varieties of beef jerky; hickory smoked, teriyaki, peppered. Granted we had to crack the windows every now and again, but overall the drive was a pleasant one.

I fell in love with Cincinnati immediately when, upon entering downtown, signs posted that parking started at $1.

OPENING COMMENTARY

My Chicago experience tells me that $1 will get one tire in a parking lot for one minute. We trekked a half mile along Vine street, towards Fountain Square, all the time being drawn in by Cornhole bags visible only at there highest arch. Upon closer inspection those bags landed on boards which lined the square for at least 50 yards. These were the social players enjoying some bag tossing with the Bengal cheerleaders. Piercing the heart of the square was a barricade set-up, with bleachers, holding in some of the best Cornholers in the world. This was the area where a World Champion would be awarded. Same day, same square, same cause for the Easter Seals, but two different competitions. Cornhole was co-existing as game and sport, a fairly new twist for Cornhole, but one that has been evolving and finding success throughout the Midwest and beginning to sprawl outside its comfort zone to the coasts.

There is a contagious excitement in the air today for the game of Cornhole. You can see it on the faces of those involved in the grass roots, you can hear it the voices of the players. The humble beginnings of the game were rooted in family outings and fanatic tailgates. In recent history the Cornhole community has turned up the competition, with leagues, tournaments and a professional circuit. The gap between backyard thrower and tournament player is widening. This progression deserves some attention as it grows steam into a gaming movement, with no apparent sign that it is slowing down.

My goal in writing a book on Cornhole is to promote the game as a whole in an effort for others to enjoy the game as much as I. Because the game and sport of Cornhole is in a budding organizational stage, there are many opinions on which path should be taken. This book does not endorse any one organizing body or builder or product. This book aims to applaud each organizing body, builder or product that seeks to spread the love of Cornhole. You will find that throughout the book I make mention of many people and organizations in the Cornhole world. I do this to paint the most complete picture of the game. If it appears I give more "face" time to any one movement, that does not signal a preference, but only that the facts presented are more voluminous.

Those who play Cornhole love the game, and are the biggest proponents to spreading the fun. The game is an easy sell. Everything about Cornhole is easy in the beginning; the rules, the play, the boards and bags. Only after pitching a few bags does one fall into an addiction that is hard to shake. Who would think that Cornhole, throwing bags in a hole; such a simple concept, could have addictive mass appeal.

HISTORY

"Thus the heavens and the earth and all their array were completed. Since on the seventh day God was finished with the work he had been doing, he rested on the seventh day from all the work he had undertaken. So God blessed the seventh day and made it holy, because on it he rested from all the work he had done in creation."

   -Genesis, Chapter 2, Verses 1-3

I DON'T IMAGINE IT TOO FAR-FETCHED for our good Lord to have rested on the seventh day enjoying a cold one and a game of Cornhole. Had Genesis gone into a bit more detail, the chapter of Cornhole's history may have been an easier sell. However, as it stands, the origin of the game of Cornhole is an enigma wrapped in a mystery. Possibly one best suited for four teenage sleuths and their dog to unravel, until now.

Many theories, ranging from roots in Germany, to Native

American settlements, to somewhere in the Midwest such as Ohio or Kentucky, filter through the Cornhole community ranks. Each offer just enough truth for a solid defense, but each contains a touch of the ridiculous that can be easily debunked. The one farce I found most fantastic was about a Bavarian cabinet maker by the name of Matthias Kuepermann, who, in 1325, grew inspiration for the game by watching boys throw stones in a hole. Unfortunately, as the story goes, for good ol' Herr Kuepermann, the Corn Laws of Britain, enacted in the 15th century, stifled corn trade and in turn the game. What really sends the story over the edge is the claim that the board-making for Cornhole was so rapid, that it led to an unnatural deforestation of Bavaria. Even though the authors wrote the tall tale in jest, elements of the story still filter through the web, as Cornhole sites copy tidbits of the story in explaining the history of the game.

Aside from Kuepermann, two other gentlemen find their way into Cornhole folklore. One is an Irish lad by the name of Jebediah McGillicuddy, not to be confused with Jebediah Springfield, founder of the Simpons' Springfield. The other legend went by William Charles Hosatch, a name better suited for the game of golf. The theories are nothing more than story telling. Though, somewhere at sometime, the stars aligned for one man, and he gave unto us the game of Cornhole. I call him a genius.

The Genius Farmer

While there is no definite history on the precise moment

in time when a genius farmer pitched the first bag, there are subtle clues that do narrow time and place. These clues are presented in the very nature that Cornhole manifests itself; with its traditions, materials and it's rules or standards. These qualities define Cornhole as a unique game, worthy of a unique history, rather than pawning off the origin on some primitive peoples that threw something into something else. The game of Cornhole deserves a genius farmer, in which, to root its traditions.

The Corntry of Origin

Cornhole achieves its name, in large part, to the material used to stuff a traditional bag, corn kernels. This material choice makes Cornhole unique. Footballs and basketballs are filled with air, and golf balls and baseballs with rubber. The material choices each game chooses aligns with the athletic feat trying to be accomplished. It just so happens that crushed corn kernels, create the right weight, feel and flight to throw at a wooden board. The game of Cornhole and corn go together like rama lama lama ka dinga da dinga dong. This relationship is crucial when assigning origin for the game of Cornhole.

Corn, in the eyes of Americans, and our friendly northern neighbor, Canada, is actually what the rest of the world calls maize. Outside our borders, corn is known as a type of grain crop, which can include maize, but is primarily referring to wheat and barley. When it comes to maize, no one touches the United States of America, where we produce nearly 335 ton a year. In comparison, Germany produces less than 1% of that total. Maize or American corn is a specialized American crop. We invest so much innovation in how we produce this crop that today, American corn touches every grocery aisle in some ingredient form or another. Furthermore, the presence of corn can be seen in animal feed and even ethanol gasoline. American corn is our baby that we have raised, altered and proudly introduced to the global marketplace. In other simplified words, America owns all things American corn. This includes the throwing bag for Cornhole, wrongly called a beanbag, more accurately called a kernel bag.

Whether you peel away the husk to an ear of American corn, or the fabric from a traditional throwing bag, you will find the same thing, the kernel. No other corn type, only maize, produces the kernel. A handful collection of these tiny natural pellets makes up the very guts of the game Cornhole. Some of the kernels are completely or partially crushed, but whole kernels still find a way to survive. Squeezing a Cornhole bag just right, one can feel the kernel outline and dimple. Cornhole bags were not filled with European corn, wheat and barley, they were filled with American corn kernels, and from these tiny wonders Cornhole received half its name.

Because maize has been globally recognized as a true American crop, then the kernel by attached association bleeds red, white and blue, and so this leaves no doubt that the first time a bag was filled with kernels, it was done so in America. Cornhole, in its material pursuits, owes a key ingredient of its origin to the American kernel.

Native Americans?

What people of America are responsible for Cornhole? Surely the Native Americans had the means to fashion such a game, where they would throw a sack of maize kernels into a hole. No one can state without reservation, that Native Americans never enjoyed a day of the pipe and some toss. I am sure the absence of television, resulted in numerous types and variations of games we see today. For example, the Mayan's played a game called pok-a-tok, using a solid rubber ball and a ring placed on a vertical pole. Much like basketball today, a score would occur when a ball would go through the ring. The game was a violent one, leading to many injuries and even death. While uncommon, the losing team on occasion would be sacrificed.

James Naismith knew of this ancient game when creating the game of basketball. He used peach baskets for goals, and defined specific rules and standards of play. The first game was played among a gym class of boys, just shy of Christmas in 1891. The game resulted in much less killing. James Naismith has been recognized by the basketball community, and rightly so, for creating the game of basketball.

While inspiration for a game may come from ancient sources, that which makes a game its own comes from its unique traditions, materials and rules. Though, one can paint a picture of Squanto air mailing his bag over Pilgrim William Bradford's blocker, during the first Thanksgiving festivities.

21

The game of Cornhole has traditionally been played to a score of 21. Some Cornhole communities rule that an exact score of 21 must be achieved for victory, while most others agree that the first to reach 21 or over is the winner. When the pace of a game needs to pick up, some play to a score of 11. Still, the 21 scoring rule remains Cornhole's standard. This rule is another example of how Cornhole is uniquely defined.

The rule of 21 debunks any Native American origin theory. The fact that the first Thanksgiving took place in 1621 is mere coincidence. The more likely explanation of the Cornhole scoring system comes from the game of horseshoes, where informal games play up to winning scores of 15 or 21, a regulation game up to 40. This pitching game reached a popular status in America during the Civil War among Union soldiers using discarded muleshoes. By 1910, horseshoes had reached such recognition that the first horseshoe-pitching tournament took place in Bronson, Kansas.

A less likely explanation comes from a European card game, 21, or as it is better known today, Blackjack. This game arrived into the United States in the 19th century, where it was rejected on the east coast as a criminal's game, passed over for the "refined" game of bridge. Blackjack (and poker for that matter) gained popularity on the riverboats that steamed along the Mississippi and Ohio Rivers. The eclectic population of New Orleans reveled in much of the gaming debauchery, but those who lived in the Corn Belt port cities played their fair share of chance games as well.

The genius farmer, who pitched that first bag, adopted the scoring system of horseshoes to Cornhole. Or in a far-fetched scenario, he was a degenerate gambler paying homage to his favorite card game. In either case, Cornhole's scoring suggests that the game came to be no earlier than 1865, and most likely sometime during the 20th century.

Plywood

The aforementioned corn in Cornhole has been discussed above. The other piece to the compound is the word "hole". Plywood, or the absence thereof, plays a big role in the naming of the game Cornhole. Plywood, like corn, is a traditional Cornhole material used to manufacture the playing surface of the game. Essentially, plywood is a series of thin wood veneers glued together. A properly sanded and painted piece of plywood, ever so gently slanted down from a 6" diameter penetrated hole, is used as a bag's hopeful home.

Plywood lends itself as the perfect material choice for a Cornhole board, offering the path of least resistance for any woodworker. The dimensions of a Cornhole board alone, 2' x 4', happen to match the measurement standard of plywood. This was no coincidence. Furthermore, the ease of attachment to a Cornhole frame and the poking of the hole are both child's play for plywood.

After all plywood is a war tested material. In the Second World War, plywood barracks housed military personnel, who rested after a long day of flying plywood gliders and riding plywood PT boats. Because of generous war funds, many times innovations in materiality are researched, refined and used for battle, before being mass marketed to the public. This certainly was true with plywood. The applied uses of plywood expanded exponentially after the war. At the war's end in 1944, 30 mills produced 1.4 billion square feet of plywood. By 1954, the number of mills more than tripled, and by 1960, 7.8 billion square feet of plywood were being produced. Plywood had now become a readily available material choice for the common man. The genius farmer, who pitched the first bag, took advantage of the post-war plywood boom, applying the material to his gaming concoction. The timing could not have been better; America had just saved the world from Nazi rule, and could once again enjoy the fruits of their sustained freedom.

Corn Belt

If Cornhole, or any game, is defined by its traditions, materials and rules, then we can say with near certainty that Cornhole is an American game. Furthermore, the scoring system and the use of a plywood-playing surface, suggest the timing of Cornhole's origin to have occurred around 1950.

The next step is to locate the exact area, where the genius farmer pitched his first bag. At the time of post-World War II America, there were 48 states in our union. Alaska and Hawaii joined the gang in 1959. The genius farmer's location can further be narrowed from the 48 states by looking within America's Corn Belt. This agriculture region is centered in Iowa and Illinois, extending to S Minnesota, SE South Dakota, E Nebraska, NE Kansas, N Missouri, Indiana and W Ohio. In the 1950's, corn acreage dominated any other crop in the Corn Belt, courtesy of fertile and deep soil with long, hot and humid summers.

Chances are the first bag was stuffed with corn kernels where kernels were most prevalent. Someone, who lives and dies corn, may find just about as many uses as he can for the crop. During one of those blazing summers, the genius farmer, kicked back a cold one and pitched his first corn-stuffed bag, somewhere in the Corn Belt of America.

Germans and Their Beer

The Corn Belt includes nine different states, each of which is included in the Midwest region of America. We, the people of the Midwest, know two types of public buildings; churches and drinking houses. Beer is the staple to any reasonable diet and a fixture at all social events. Cornhole is no different when it comes to that relationship with beer.

Beer is to the Cornhole player what spinach is to Popeye; a nutritional necessity for peak performance. The Cornhole player owes a debt of gratitude to one, some or all of the following fine men; Joseph Schlitz, Frederick Pabst, Adolphus Busch, Eberard Anheuser, Adolph Coors and Frederick Miller, each of whom founded a brewery and each of whom is a German immigrant.

In a hundred year span, from 1820 to 1920, the United States of America welcomed nearly six million German immigrants to its shores. A vast majority came between the years of 1840 to 1880, which happened to be America's largest immigrant group of that time. Germans found preference in New York and Baltimore, and further inland to the Midwest cities of Chicago, Cincinnati, Cleveland, St. Louis and Milwaukee (also known as the German Athens). Due to the large number of German immigrants that settled the rural heartland of the Midwest, they accounted for over a third of the agriculture produced in that region. Aside from having a dominant influence on farming and brewing, German immigrants affected the recreational climate as well. In fact, it was the German immigrant who popularized bowling in the Midwest.

By 1900, the population of Cincinnati, Cleveland and Milwaukee were more than 40% German American. Of those three, only one fully embraced the Corn Belt lifestyle, by hugging western Ohio. That city, one of German beer and American Corn, is Cincinnati.

Cincinnati and Cornhole

In the early 19th century, German immigrants began populating Cincinnati to the point that the city became known as America's first boomtown. Cincinnati's size and wealth rivaled the coastal cities. Its location on the Ohio-Kentucky border, along the Ohio River, made the city an epicenter for travelers, sharing commerce and ideas primarily by steamship and railroad.

By the 1950's a new transportation line was taking shape throughout America; the Interstate Highway System. Dwight D. Eisenhower, (one of two Presidents with German ancestry, the other being Herbert Hoover) as Supreme Commander of the Allied Forces, gained respect for Germany's Autobahn, as a viable tool for national defense. As president, Eisenhower set out to create a similar network for America. One north-south interstate, number 75, divides the city of Cincinnati, between what is known as the West-Side and the East-Side. This split is not purely geographic, but has cultural divides as well.

West-Siders enjoy the outdoor barbecue scene and Bengal football, whereas an East-Sider might indulge in some sushi and a ballet. The West is rooted in deep family ties, where generations have lived one after the other. The East is comprised of a younger group of implants looking to start a family. The West more blue collar, the East more hip, and the contrasts go on. You get the point. In general, the rivalry between the two sides stems from a conservative approach to life as opposed to a more liberal one.

No surprise that the game of Cornhole has its foundation in the West side of town. West-Siders are fanatics when it comes to sports and love their neighborhood drinking hole. Everyone knows what parish they reside and each parish has a summer festival to establish that fact. Every West-Sider has a story of their grandpa pitching a bag back in the day. Most might claim that their grandpa founded the game. And they might be right. Any name a West-Sider gives is better than McGillicuddy or Hosatch.

Also, it is no coincidence that the two governing bodies of Cornhole, the American Cornhole Organization and the American Cornhole Association, were both founded in the Cincinnati area.

A Cornhole Origin

In conclusion, the origin of Cornhole took place on Cincinnati's west-side during the 1950's, something any West-Sider could have relayed in one sentence. It is here where the game of Cornhole defined itself through traditions, materials, and rules. After sifting through American history and other potpourri, the conclusion to a West-Sider might be somewhat melodramatic. At least now they have some ammo from those pesky pitchers from Kentucky lying claim to the game, or worse yet, those yuppies from the City of Chicago.

"The Colonial War of Liberation was won on the village greens by pitchers of horse hardware."
   -Duke of Wellington

Inspirations for Cornhole

Cornhole is classified as a tossing or lawn game. The family is comprised of backyard golf, bocce, boule lyonnaise, bowls, cherokee marbles, horseshoes, kubb, ladder golf, ladder toss, lawn darts, mölkky, pétanque, quoits, roque, snake pit, trac ball and washers, among others. Each game within this family demands that a player accurately throw a projectile at a goal. Traditionally, these games are played between two people or two teams of two. Furthermore, the family of toss games is not timed and plays to a specific score.

In the timeline of game tossing history, Cornhole is a relatively new entrant. Two games that paved the way for

Cornhole were horseshoes and quoits. The latter, quoits, entails throwing rings of metal or rope over or near a spike known as a hob. English nobility and aristocrats loved the game. By the 15th century quoits had become well-organized within pubs and taverns. The early colonists to America brought quoits and horseshoes with them. But by the time we fought for our Independence in 1775, horseshoes was primarily played and quoits was on its way to extinction.

Horseshoes draws its inspiration, as a game, from the Olympic sport of discus throwing. Greeks idolized their Olympic heroes and made every attempt to imitate them. However, the average Greek could not afford to purchase a discus, so they used a horseshoe as a substitute. Tossing horseshoes began as purely a distance contest. Only after a stake was introduced did the game transform into one of accuracy. Our forefathers were known to play the game and our soldiers from every major campaign spread the game across the nation. By the early 20th century, horseshoes became organized in America, in large part due to the formation of a governing body (the National Horseshoe Pitchers' Association), adoption of standard rules, and the manufacture of standard pitching shoes.

SOCIAL IMPACT

"We're not here for the game. The game is nothing. The game is crap. The game makes me sick. The real reason we Americans put up with sports is for this: Behold, the tailgate party. The pinnacle of human achievement. Since the dawn of parking lots, man has sought to fill his gut with food and alcohol in anticipation of watching others exercise."

- Homer Simpson

"T<small>HUD!</small>"

My father rose from a sleep, with his top half straightened perpendicular to the bed. Moments passed, then another thud confirmed that he was not dreaming. Rising to the window of his cottage, in the early ante meridiem hours, he witnessed his first Cornhole game.

I visited the cottage, on Delavan Lake in Wisconsin, a couple weeks after this event. We sat outside the red painted lake home, facing a park that centered a community of summer homes, picturesquely placed among curving roads. Most homes display welcoming signs, that often contain some kind of word play, like *Come on Inn* or *Relax Inn*. In the summertime, the lake awakes from hibernation, as fish, mosquitoes, squirrels and the assembled masses all come out to play. The older folk grow weary of the college kids that rent a home and fill the park nightlife with an occasional golf cart joyride, and in the case of the thuds, the game of Cornhole. My father reasoned that the kids did not get their fill at the North Shore Bar up the road, and settled into a late night game of thudhole, as he might call it. I laughed. I had played the game a few times while tailgating, so I attempted to explain the appeal. Telling a tired and irritated man can be fruitless, but showing him, by buying him a Cornhole board and bags, proved to be the trick.

Before long my father had mastered a sliding technique into the hole. The family and extended joined the fun, and now Cornhole is a fixture at any Rogers' gathering. Can't say he is thrilled about the occasional midnight thud, but at least now he understands.

The Social Scene

Cornhole's impact has reached the very social fabric of various communities, positively enhancing the well being of individuals and families. The appeal to the game is its ease of play and the ability of any age and gender to participate. This has led to Cornhole being featured through fundraisers and neighborhood gatherings, as an innovative tool to garner people's attention towards a cause or event. To a newcomer, the game is curious and because Cornhole is so easy to initially grasp, that person is drawn in and kept in.

Cornhole is beginning to socially creep into arenas and forums that are not traditional Cornhole markets. For instance, recently, my wife showed me that Cornhole had found its way to the pages of Real Simple magazine. This periodical targets women with information on home keeping, childcare, cooking, and now Cornhole. The picture displayed a standard issue Cornhole board and bags, not the cheap looking plastic version. They even call the game Cornhole, not Bags, so good for them. Cornhole is also finding its way to the movies, television and music. This chapter will take a look at some of these elements as Cornhole sets a societal foundation.

Eventually, I want to see Homer pitch a bag. The Simpsons have been lampooning American society for almost 25 years, touching on nearly every aspect of American culture. Cornhole will know its made the big time when it is featured in this animated sitcom.

Cornhole and Fundraising (and Beer)

Where there is a cause there is a fundraiser. Non-profit organizations rely on the generosity of the private and public sectors to donate time and money to fight a myriad of causes, from political to medical. Pleads may take the form of an event fundraiser such as formal dinners, walkathons or benefit concerts. The fundraiser event not only raises money, but gives an organization the forum to educate the participants about their cause. Sports play a big role as a draw for charity fundraisers. Some of the most common sports used are running, golfing and more recently Cornhole.

Cornhole has many advantages as the sport of choice for a fundraiser event. First, all ages and types can play Cornhole. Some may be turned off from running a 5k or lugging clubs for 18 holes, particularly if golf is foreign to them. But Cornhole has a low barrier to entry, where anyone at anytime can grab a bag and get the gist of the toss. Cornhole also lends itself to more exposure of the charitable cause. Donor cultivation, or relationship building, is the foundation of charity work. On the golf course, a charity director may only see the players before and after the round. On the Cornhole boards, the director can be in constant contact with the audience, taking pledges, names for mailers and newsletters, running raffles and in general, building a rapport with donors. Cost is another reason that Cornhole is appealing. There are no individual green fees or equipment rentals, just a comparatively small rental fee for boards & bags, that everyone uses. Space is yet another advantage to Cornhole. Planning a route for a 5k involves closing down streets and working with the local governance to do so. Cornhole needs only a lawn, an empty lot or indoor facility with a ceiling height greater than 15 feet. Finally, like a 5k, but unlike a golf event, the sport of Cornhole can be easily viewed by spectators. Family and friends of players can rally boardside, which concurrently increases eyes on the charitable cause.

In recent years, charity directors have become privy to the

advantages of a Cornhole event. It comes as no surprise that Cornhole is now a leader as the sport of choice for a fundraising event.

Cornhole and Tailgating (and Beer)

Tailgating, more specifically, college football tailgating, has played a significant role in increasing Cornhole awareness and popularity. The tailgate is the ultimate sports social event taking place outside of stadiums nationwide before, during and after the game. Upon arriving several hours before kickoff, the tailgate of the vehicle will be opened to access food set-up, sitting accommodations and parking lot games. Together with a sea of people, the tailgating party begins.

From its beginning, tailgating has been the understood pre-game activity within the subculture of fanatics. As the tailgate became refined to a complete social experience, some began to participate at a strictly party level, ignoring the actual main event inside the stadium. By 1993 the tailgate had achieved such powerful status within the college ranks that ESPN set-up shop; crew, gear and commentators reported and analyzed live from a portable stage at the heart of the tailgate party. This pre-game show, known as College GameDay, and the star Lee Corso, still travel to a new college tailgating experience every football week.

Tailgate nation coordinates feverishly to supply enough food, drink and comfort to survive any weather conditions. One item that has become a must for the tailgate is a set of Cornhole boards. The game lends itself to the tailgate experience. Being a lawn game, the play area and set-up can easily be handled within the rows of cars. And because the game is foldable, the Cornhole set is travel friendly.

Every NCAA Division I college participates in four road football games. Often times the team's most fervent supporters make the journey to hostile territory. That's four different places those fans have where they can make a lasting impression to their hosts. Many do not like to see the Ohio State Buckeyes roll into town, but one thing they do like is the Cornhole set that the Buckeye fans bring with them. Fans from colleges in Ohio, Kentucky, Indiana and Illinois have been spreading the love of Cornhole across the nation through the tailgate. The game is easily imitable and visible and therefore can never be kept a guarded secret. Colleges from around the nation have jumped on the Cornhole bandwagon and it comes as no surprise that the most common decoration of a board is a college logo with team colors. The tailgate has proven to be the conduit through which Cornhole has become noticed.

Cornhole and Bars (and Beer)

The tavern, pub, alehouse, honky tonk, saloon, watering hole, and God Bless if you frequented a speakeasy in the Roaring '20's, but anyway you say it, the bar is the home of our social life just as the Church is the home of our spiritual life. Other than the allure of killing a few brain cells, a bars underlying main draw is its low barrier to entry. Almost everyone is welcome, all types enter through its doors, in fact, legally speaking about 70% of Americans can walk right up to the bar and order an alcoholic beverage. That's it, nothing to it. Challenges arise once inside a bar such as getting a phone number, controlling restroom stops, and later in the night, the challenge of walking, but the low barrier to entry at the beginning of any bar visit remains.

It makes sense that the bar would surround itself with other low barrier to entry doodads, to keep patrons inside its doors. This includes, but is not limited to, darts, arcade & video games, trivia contests, shuffleboard and pool. Each is designed for anyone to play, while enjoying a cold one and talking with their buds. The games are not meant to be overly aggressive and competitive, instead they serve as an outlet for fun and banter. Not coincidently, most can be played with one hand on the bottle. Not only can Cornhole be played with one hand on the bottle, some may argue that the counter weight is actually strategically advantageous.

It comes as no surprise that the game of Cornhole has infiltrated bars in Cincinnati, spreading throughout Ohio, Indiana, Kentucky, reaching up to Chicago and growing momentum outside the Midwest, sprinkling from sea to shining sea. Some of the original Cincinnati bars to feature Cornhole include Sneaky Pete's, Logos Sports Bar and Century Inn.

In 1970, Benny Binion, along with his son Jack, premiered to the Vegas public, the first World Series of Poker (WSOP). Benny was introduced to a Las Vegas pre-Bugsy Siegel, where Reno still held an edge as the West's gambling Mecca. In 1951, Binion decided to purchase the Eldorado Club and Apache Hotel. He made the casino his own with high limit betting,

SOCIAL IMPACT

limousine pick-up for customers and free drinks to players. Benny named this casino Binion's Horseshoe. By 1970, Las Vegas had leap-frogged Reno, and Binion decided to host the first WSOP Main Event featuring Texas Hold'em. Two hurdles stood in his way, poker tables required valuable slot machine space and cheating frequently occurred. Concerning the later, Cornhole has not become notorious for its cheats. However, the term "Kitten" has been used to call out a pro-caliber Cornholer who masks his professional status in order to enter and collect on an amateur tournament. In a bar environment, sacrificing patron drinking space for Cornhole can be difficult to swallow. Instead, bar owners may opt for the coin-operated video game "Bags". This electronic game by Incredible Technologies, creator of Golden Tee, takes only fifty square feet of realty. Some bars are blessed with ample parking or patio area, where boards and bags can be played outdoors. When space becomes a concern, Midwest bar owners are doing what Benny did 40 years ago. Binion knew if he promoted a tournament, not only would competitors come for a piece of the pie, but spectators would follow. He called on the help of odds maker, Jimmy 'the Greek' Snyder to promote his event. Similarly, bar owners are finding that promoting a tournament is far more profitable than just setting up boards for curious patrons. Cornhole tournaments have become increasingly popular, particularly in the Midwest. [See chapter, Running a Cornhole Tournament]

Cornhole the Movie

Cornhole hit the silver screen in 2010 with "Cornhole the Movie." The writer and director of the film, Timothy Clark, was welcomed back to the Cincinnati area where he graduated high school at St. Xavier in 1988. Pre-production and casting began in 2007 with the full support and participation of the Cornhole community. Those from Cincinnati (or their bums) may recognize the bleachers borrowed from the Norwood baseball fields or more likely might notice the interior shots of Shimmers Tavern, Logo's Sports Bar or Sneaky Pete's.

The film shot for 18 days with a total budget of $100,000. The result was a hybrid of the ridiculous from the movie "Best in Show" with the silliness of "Dodgeball", in what can best be described as a mockumentary. Clarke's wife, Elaine Mello, stars in the film of four teams and their unique paths to Cornhole's National Championship event. Cameos included ACO's president Frank Geers as the "torch bearer" and professional Cornholer Steve Vanderver who won his way into the movie.

The movie served as another avenue for Cornhole and its proponents to share the addiction of the game to others, in an entertaining fashion. Below are my top five quotes from "Cornhole the Movie":

5. "Does my mere presence make you want to buy a vibrator?" - Gina Rosenstones
4. Commenting on Buddy's cornholing, "The Lord has actually improved his game by about 14%."
   - Delmar Gladstone

SOCIAL IMPACT

3. "The crotch is power." - Gina Rosenstones
2. Explaining his Cornhole sacrifices, "I've given up my family, when I converted from Catholicism over to Judaism ... I'll see my family again some day -- Heaven or I don't know -- grocery store." - Noel
1. "God loves a Cornhole player, Amen!" - Stew Neagen

National Cornhole Day
July 4, 1776, American man wins independence.
July 20, 1969, American man lands on moon.
June 27, 2009, American man throws bag into hole.

The game of Cornhole left a mark on our Gregorian calendar, when the American Cornhole Organization (ACO) established the last Saturday in June as National Cornhole Day. Rocky Conteduca, Las Vegas, Nevada ACO representative, pitched the idea to ACO leadership. Rocky had seen for himself the power of Cornhole in his own neighborhood after throwing a tournament. Everyone came together, played together and have since established growing relationships. Why couldn't this work in other neighborhood pockets throughout the nation?

The idea was received and executed enthusiastically. The ACO kicked off the day with a HoleHeadz Festival for that weekend in Carrolton, Kentucky. The Cornhole community encouraged everyone to set-up boards and let their bags fly, in an effort to attract others to the game. So if you are looking for a reason to rally the neighbors with some grill and drinks, make sure to mark the last Saturday in June for a Cornhole extravaganza.

Cornhole's Band - May's Gone

"Check. Check one. Sibilance. Sibilance. Check. Check two. Sibilance. Sibilance. And now introducing Cornhole's very own, May's Gone. On guitar from Chillicothe, Ohio; Marc Secoy - fellow founding member, on the bass, Jarret Kelley - manning the other guitar; Tim Hull - on drums, the younger brother; Jon Hull - and rounding up the band on vocals; Ashley Foster."

If you have gone to an American Cornhole Organization (ACO) sponsored event in Kentucky, Ohio, Wisconsin or South Carolina, chances are you are familiar with May's Gone. They have formed a relationship with Frank Geers and the ACO, recently performing at such Cornhole events as the IceHole Classic, Brew City Bags Bash, Cornhole de Mayo, Holeheadz Festival and the Tailgate Bash in Fountain Square. Aside from following Cornhole at live venues, May's Gone has also performed overlays for Cornhole highlight reels.

However, the band is not exclusively Cornhole, nor do they have any campy or cheesy songs on Cornhole. If you have heard the "Cornhole Song", then you are actually listening to the band duo of Rhett&Link. Their spoof is creative and hilarious, and comes highly recommended. In the case of May's Gone, the band has roots in jazz, marching, bluegrass, rock, pop and classical all aligning for a unique alternative/indie rock sound.

Buttonfind

The Alcatraz prison held some of the most notorious criminals from 1930 to 1960. Among Al Capone, Birdman, and George "Machine Gun" Kelly, a man by the name of Jim Quillen, made the Rock, his home. One infraction or another may lead an inmate to solitary confinement, where they hole up in a 6' x 6' miniature cell, with no furniture and no light. On occasion, Quillen found himself alone in this dark abyss where a man could go crazy, losing all track of time and place. As the four dark walls seemed to close upon him, Quillen invented a strange way to pass the time and keep his sanity. He would flip a single button into the air, allow the button to drop and settle, before bending to his knees and sweeping his arms to find the button. Once found, Quillen would flip the button once again into the air and repeat his search. Every time Quillen flipped a button, he honed his finding skill, maybe changing his technique, in an effort to snuff out the button faster and more efficiently. Each flip, the button would land a tad differently, rolling off along a subtle grade in the concrete floor. His game was so easy to play, yet this simple challenge kept him mentally strong and provided for him a touch of amusement in an otherwise impossible situation.

I imagine Buttonfind doesn't have much marketable appeal outside the prison solitary confinement crowd. But games that seem so simple to master, have nuances that *confound a player into an addiction of playing hours on end.*

In much the same way, Cornhole at first glance seems an easy enough challenge, certainly easy to learn the rules and objectives. However, it is the allure to a repetitive process, throwing bag after bag, which keeps us playing through the night, knowing we can improve our pitching and strategies. Every throw a tad different, maybe to adjust for an opponent's bag or counter a cross wind outdoors. Cornhole allows itself to seem easy to beginners, the equivalent of a nightcrawler to a fish, as the game hooks its prey.

CORNHOLE RULES & REGULATIONS

"Meatloaf, smeatloaf, double beatloaf. I hate meatloaf."
  - Randy from *"A Christmas Story"*

THE RULES AND REGULATIONS OF CORNHOLE can vary by region, by state, even by neighborhood. This in one reason why ACA's President, Mike Whitton, established his association, in an effort to standardize the rules. However, this in no way should impede on your ability to customize the game for your enjoyment. The standards do give individuals a basis to resolve any argument and they provide for concrete regulations on what to follow within a tournament or league. They do not stop you from having house rules that fit your style. Furthermore, they do not hinder any fun twist you may add to the game.

Think about your monthly card game. The first time you rounded up the crew, you probably let everyone know about your house rules. For instance, you can only raise the pot once or the Joker counts as a fifth ace. As players pass around the deck to call there variation of poker, they may state rules for that hand, such as 'deuces wild', 'Jacks or better / trips to win' or the Queen of Spades face up kills the game. These nuances keep the game fresh and exciting. However, try imposing your will of the rules, in a poker tournament and you will be kicked to the curb. You had better know the rules of the game your playing before you sit down to a felt table in a competitive environment.

Cornhole is no different. Within the confines of your friends and family relaxing in your backyard, your house rules stand. But if you enter a Cornhole game at a bar, tailgate, tournament or league where personal preference may vary, then it is a good idea to know what rules and regulations everyone is expected to follow.

There are two primary rules and regulations standards that are followed in the game of Cornhole today. One set comes from the American Cornhole Organization (ACO) and the other from the American Cornhole Association (ACA). Both are fairly similar, so where there are differences I have noted them. Also, you will find at the end of this chapter, a couple variations of the game, such as ideas for three-man play, as well as some commonly used house rules that players may choose to incorporate into their game play.

CORNHOLE RULES & REGULATIONS

Cornhole Equipment

Before you can pitch that first bag you need to acquire some Cornhole equipment. This includes two Cornhole boards and two sets of four, Cornhole bags.

Cornhole Boards

The graph below compares an ACO sanctioned board with an ACA one. As you can see, when it comes to the Cornhole, all agree that you shouldn't mess with 6" in diameter. [See Figure 3.0]

	ACO	ACA
Material	5/8" Baltic Birch plywood	1/2" plywood
Coat finish	Clear Ultra Violet	High gloss paint
Board dimensions	47-1/2" x 23-1/2"	48" x 24"
Hole diameter	6" diameter	6" diameter
Hole location from top	Centered 8-7/8"	Centered 9"
Hole location from sides	11-3/4" to center	12" to center
Board front height	3"	2-1/2"
Board back height	12"	12"
Back leg angle with board	109 degrees	90 degrees

Cornhole Bags

The graph below compares an ACO sanctioned bag with an ACA one. As you can see, when it comes to the square, all agree that you shouldn't mess with 6" x 6" specification.

	ACO	**ACA**
Material	fabric squares	fabric squares
Stitching	nylon double stitched	double stitched
Square measures	6" x 6"	6" x 6"
Bag filling	PET Resin	Corn feed
Amount of bag filling	2 cups	2 cups
Weight of bag filling	0.915 to 0.935 lbs*	between 14-16 oz

*14.64 to 14.96 oz

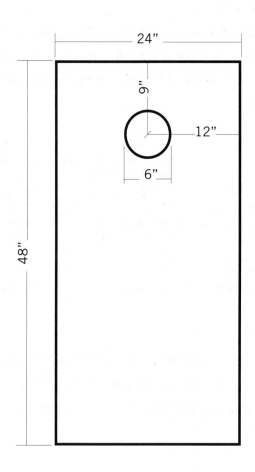

Figure 3.0: The Cornhole board

CORNHOLE RULES & REGULATIONS

Court Layout for Cornhole Play

So now that you have the equipment needed, you can place your goods onto the court. A Cornhole court consists of two (2) Cornhole boards and (2) sets of four Cornhole bags. Each set of bags should be of a different color. The court also consists of (4) pitchers' boxes and foul lines. As you read the rest of this section, follow along with [Figure 3.1] particularly for dimensions and pitchers' boxes.

Find a flat to relatively flat and level surface to set-up your boards. The area can be indoors or out. If indoors try to play in an area where you have at least 15 feet of vertical clearance. If out, try to set-up the boards in the north-south setting to minimize the effect of the sun. The court is a rectangular area. Make sure to give yourself enough room to fit one of the following dimensions.

ACO - 8' wide by a minimum of 42' long.
ACA - 10' wide by a minimum of 45' long.

If you plan to set-up multiple boards, give yourself 10-12 feet between board edges to allow for comfortable play for each game.

The pitcher's box is the area where the tosser will throw his bag. When pitching a bag the tosser must stay within the box. The area of the box is a 4' x 3' rectangle. The 4' length extends 3' from the board while remaining parallel to the board. The 4' length starts at the front of the board and ends at the back, matching the 4' length of the board.

The foul lines are defined as the front edge of the Cornhole board. The distance of one person's foul line to his opponents is determined by the level of play. In competitive play the front of the boards, and by default, the foul lines, should be 27' apart. An amateur game may choose to play at 24' and a junior may play at 20' per the ACO or 18' per the ACA. You may find, however, that most amateurs do end up playing at 27' apart as well.

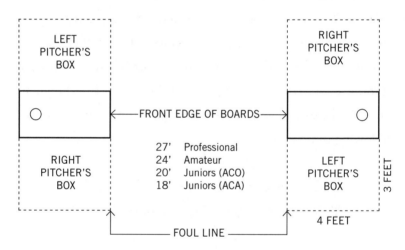

Figure 3.1: The Cornhole court

Preparation and Maintenance

Now that you have your equipment all set-up, it is time to prep the area. Both the ACO and ACA agree that the playing conditions should be made as perfect as possible. The responsibility rests on the players to check the conditions and make changes as required. Anything that might distract a contestant during play should be recognized and solved. Particularly, make sure the boards are in alignment and that the pitching boxes are clear of debris.

During the course of play, the boards may skew and angle, depending on the surface they rest upon. You are allowed to realign them with the consent of your opponent or tournament official.

When it comes to the consumption of drinks, Mike Whitton, President of the ACA suggests that, "a beer in your other hand helps balance your throw." Cornhole and beer are practically related. However, when the bags are flying your way, keep your beer off the board or anywhere near the playing surface. The ACO recommends keeping the drink in a 'safe zone'. I believe the hand to be the 'safest zone' of any man's beer. Should be noted that one caveat in the ACO's rules do not allow drinks during play for Pro-Sanctioned events.

PLAYING CORNHOLE: SINGLES

First to pitch & first position

Cornhole can be played in a singles format or doubles. In an effort to demonstrate singles play, let us follow a game between Jack Bauer and Chuck Norris. As Chuck flips a coin in the air Jack exclaims, "tails never fails and either do I." The coin lands eagle face up. With this small victory, Jack decides to stand in the right pitcher's box and pitch first. Both Jack and Chuck start by pitching at the same board.

Alternating throws and positions

Jack kicks things off, then Chuck let's his first bag fly. They alternate throwing their bags until each has thrown four each. A Cornholer is allowed 15 seconds to throw a bag (20 seconds under the ACA), but neither Jack nor Chuck takes that long, as eventually all eight bags make the hole. The first frame (or inning or cornrow) ends in a wash. For frame two, Jack and Chuck walk to the other board, and now Chuck pitches from the right pitcher's box.

Fouls

Since no one scored in the last frame, Jack is first to throw. As he stands in the left pitcher's box, a call from CTU distracts him. He attempts to have a conversation in 15 seconds. As the clock ticks to 16, the official (or police) calls a foul on Jack. This was a bad move by the official. Jack stares down the official with a dead glare until the call is reversed. He proceeds to throw a Cornhole. Chuck throws next, but is called for a foul, after his foot crosses the foul line. This was another bad move. Chuck roundhouse kicks the official, and again a foul is reversed. The official is having a long frame. Chuck proceeds to throw a Cornhole.

Other fouls that the official dare not call may include the following:
- A bag pitched when a player starts or steps completely outside the pitcher's box before releasing the bag;
- A bag pitched from a different pitcher's box than the first bag;

- Any bag that contacts the court or ground before resting on the board surface or in the hole;
- Any bag that strikes a defined object such as a tree limb, wire, indoor ceiling, etc.;
- A player removes a bag on the board before the score for that frame is determined.

If a foul occurs and stands, then that bag is removed from the playing area and all affected bags are returned to their previous position. The foul bag receives a zero count. For example, a foul bag that knocks another bag into the hole, results in the foul bag being removed and the bag in the hole is put back to its previous position on the board. Another example would be, if a foul bag knocks off a bag already on the board. In this case, the knocked bag would be placed back onto the board. Any protest can be brought to the official in a non-roundhouse manner, where he will make the final ruling.

Scoring

Finally, in frame three, some scoring happens. Chuck has thrown two in the hole, one on the board and one on the ground. Jack countered with three on the board, and one in the hole.

A bag that enters completely into the hole counts as three points and is often called a Cornhole. The bag counts as a Cornhole if you throw it into the hole or the bag is knocked into the hole. When Jack and Chuck play, sometimes so many bags enter the hole that they stack, making it difficult for that last bag to fully enter. In this scenario, the bags that have already entered the hole can be cleared for future Cornholes.

Any bag that doesn't make it into the hole, but remains on the board counts as one point and is sometimes referred to as an Ace. However, any bag that comes to rest on the board after hitting the ground or any bag that is touching both ground and board is a foul and should be removed.

Adding up the total points for frame three would result in the following:

    Norris: 3 + 3 + 1 + 0 = 7 points
    Bauer: 3 + 1 + 1 + 1 = 6 points

Cancellation System

The ACA recommends a cancellation scoring system. This means that Cornholes and Aces are cancelled out separately. Adding a player's 'Cornhole score' plus 'Ace score' results in his final score of the frame. In this case, Jack is able to cancel out one of Chuck's Cornholes. Chuck is left with one Cornhole for a 'Cornhole score' of 3, as calculated below:

    Bauer: Jack's lone Cornhole is cancelled.
                   Cornhole score = 0
    Norris: After cancelling one Cornhole, Chuck is left with one. Cornhole score = 3

Jack has thrown three bags on the board. One of those points cancels out Chuck's bag on the board. Jack beats Chuck in the 'Ace score' by 2, as calculated below.

Bauer: One of Jack's Aces cancels with Chuck's lone Ace. Ace score = 1 + 1 = 2
Norris: His lone Ace is cancelled. Ace score = 0.

The final score of the frame is Chuck 3 and Jack 2, as calculated below:

Bauer: Cornhole score of 0 + Ace score of 2 = 2
Norris: Cornhole score of 3 + Ace score of 0 = 3

Differential System

The ACO recommends a negation or differential system, where the total scores are subtracted, with the winner of the frame receiving all the points. Using this format Chuck would receive 1 point to Jack's 0, (7 - 6 = 1) as calculated below:

Norris: 3 + 3 + 1 + 0 = 7 points
Bauer: 3 + 1 + 1 + 1 = 6 points
1 point

Sometimes this format is referred to as cancellation as well, because one total score is cancelling out another. This form of cancelling has become the most popular among Cornhole players, in large part due to its ease of calculating. The odds are good that if you are playing Cornhole you are using the

Differential system. Still, it is always a good idea to make sure what system is being used.

Rally System

A third way to keep score is called a rally system, where the totals for each player count towards the score of the frame. No cancellation of any form is taken into account. Using this format Chuck would receive 7 points to Jack's 6.

Of the three, the rally format makes for a much quicker match. A good Cornhole game will rarely use the rally format, because realistically the game can be wrapped up in two frames. This format is best suited for juniors as a fun way to learn Cornhole.

No matter what scoring system you choose to use, it is always a good idea to pay close attention to the score at all times. Some boards come customized with a scoring tab along a back edge. A separate visible scoreboard of any nature will also work. Good practice suggests that each frame score and total score be verbally announced before pitching the next frame. In the event, that a score can not be agreed upon, a tournament judge will make a final decision. If there is no judge present, you are probably playing with friends and/or family. In this case, just let your cousin Billy have that extra point, for crying out loud.

Winning Honors

With his score in frame 3, Chuck has earned himself honors for frame 4. This means Chuck gets to pitch first. This can be an advantage, as it allows Chuck to block the hole if desired, or set the pace with a Cornhole. Honors are always awarded to the player who scored in the previous frame.

In frame four, both Jack and Chuck are back to form, Cornholing four bags a piece. The frame is a wash and nobody scores.

ACO: If nobody is honored, in that, the frame is a wash with no score, then honors revert back to whomever had them last. Since nobody scored in frame 4, Chuck will be first to throw in frame 5.

ACA: If neither pitcher scores, then the player who pitched second in the preceding frame will have honors the next frame. Nobody scored in frame 4. Therefore, Jack, who pitched second in frame 4, will pitch first in frame 5.

Game Length

A Cornhole game is played until a player reaches 21 (or more) at the completion of an inning. The winner need not win by two or more points or land exactly on 21.

Heading into frame 30, the score is Jack 20 to Chuck's 18. A truly epic battle. When the bag dust settles, Chuck has pitched three in the hole and one on the board. For his part, Jack hit the hole twice and the board twice. The scoring for frame 30, looks like this:

Norris: 3 + 3 + 3 + 1 = 10 points
Bauer: 3 + 3 + 1 + 1 = 8 points

Using the ACA's cancellation system, Jack would receive 1 point for his surviving Ace and Chuck would receive 3 points for his surviving Cornhole. Frame 30 scoring and total is as follows:

    Norris: 3 + 18 = 21
    Bauer: 1 + 20 = 21

In the case of a tie, play continues until Jack or Chuck scores higher at the end of a frame.

It is important to note, that the game is not over until all 8 bags are pitched in the frame. Therefore, although a player may be first to reach 21, or exceed, within a frame, that frame must fully complete before a score can be established.

However, these two gentlemen are scoring using ACO's differential canceling system. Therefore, the scoring for frame 30 goes to Chuck and looks like this:

    Norris: 3 + 3 + 3 + 1 = 10 points
    Bauer: 3 + 3 + 1 + 1 = 8 points
                                   2 points

Adding frame 30 to the scores, results in both player's tied at 20 as follows:

    Norris: 2 + 18 = 20
    Bauer: 0 + 20 = 20

Since every frame either results in a wash or a score for one player, per the ACO rules, then the next player to score wins this game. A tie is not possible using the differential scoring system.

Cornhole Skunk

Skunk in any context is not pleasant, certainly not for those being skunked. A skunk occurs when you are defeating someone so handily that your opponent cannot score and you rack up a good chunk of points. If a skunk is achieved the player who shut-out his opponent is the victor. The amount you must accumulate before your opponent scores is debatable. Usually the skunk rule defaults to the house. And that being the case, a traditional Midwest house game ends with a skunk score of 11 (or more) points scored before the other player scores. Here are some other skunk standards:

ACA: Skunk score is 7 (or more) to 0
ACO: Skunk score is 13 (or more) to 0

You might find as your skill level progresses that the ACA's standard is a bit low. The ACO's "13" mark is more reasonable, as a player may get hot and Cornhole four bags in a frame to get himself right back into the action.

However, the ACO notes that when it comes to sanctioned events, skunk rules do not apply. This makes sense, because momentum shifts can easily turn what seemed to be a lopsided score to dead even. This is particularly true when you are dealing with two high-caliber competitors.

Cornhole Etiquette

When discussing etiquette, remember that this is not golf or a dinner party. The game is to be enjoyed in a light atmosphere of good drink and food and friends. Still keep two things in mind when playing Cornhole - 'be cool' and 'don't be that guy'. The following is a list of actions you can take to show your Cornhole sportsmanship:

- Do not make any disturbing movements or noises that distracts your opponent
- Do not roundhouse kick your opponent
- Keep the board in play clear of any objects, including beer
- Keep the pace of the game
- No cell phones, OMG.
- Do not use abusive language
- Do not let your shadow drop within your opponents pitching line
- Do not interrogate your opponent

PLAYING CORNHOLE: DOUBLES

Much of what you have learned above will be applied to doubles play. The following instruction on how to play doubles will pinpoint what differences may pop up when introducing a partner. The most important factor to consider in doubles play is positioning.

Jack calls Chloe and orders her to come to the Cornhole boards immediately. Meanwhile, Trivette pulls up in his pick-up truck ready to partner up with Chuck. Chuck and Jack continue to face each other and stand at one board. Their partners, Chloe and Trivette stand opposite them at the other board. This means that for team 'Rangers', if Chuck is in the left pitcher's box then Trivette stands in the right pitcher's box.

The players with the bags are referred to as the "headboard" and their partners the "footboard." It is good practice for the footboard players to announce the score before picking up the bags and throwing the next frame.

Just like singles, Chuck and Jack alternate throws until all 8 bags are pitched. The winner of the frame determines which team member receives honors. In frame 1, Jack scores 10 to Chuck's 8, and is rewarded with 2 points for team '24'. Chloe will be first to throw against Trivette in frame two. Game play continues this way, keeping in mind the rules and regulations set forth in the singles discussion of this chapter.

PLAYING CORNHOLE: 3-PLAYER GAMES

Cutthroat, Version 1

The designation "cutthroat" is used for any game where three players compete and each is looking out for themselves, no teaming. You may have used the term in the game of pool or bridge.

For the Cornhole version of the game only Cornholes

count and receive a score of 3. A bag anywhere else scores nothing. Each player throws all four bags, before the next player proceeds. After a player throws all four bags, he counts the number of Cornholes and multiplies by 3. That score remains his, unless the next player matches or exceeds that number of Cornholes. If the next player succeeds in doing that then the points are transferred to him, along with whatever the next player scored. After the three players had a turn of throwing their four bags the round ends. The next round starts with the player with the highest point total, followed by the runner-up and ending with the player with the least points from the previous round. In the case of a tie, the players revert to the previous round's order. The game is won when a player has reached 21 or higher at the end of a round.

Here is an example of Rounds 1 & 2:

Peter: Throws one Cornhole for a score of 3.
Paul: Throws one Cornhole for a score of 3. Because he matched Peter's pitch, he steals Peter's points as well. Paul now has 6 points. Peter now reverts to 0 points.
Mary: Throws two Cornholes for a score of 6. Because she exceeded Paul's number of Cornholes, Mary steals Paul's 6 points. Mary finishes round 1 with 12 points and the two men finish with 0 points.

Mary starts round 2 since she is the high scorer. Peter and Paul are tied at 0, so the previous round order dictates how they will pitch in round 2.

Mary: Throws two Cornholes again for a score of 6. For the time being, Mary has 12 + 6 = 18 points.

Peter: Throws two Cornholes for a score of 6. Because he matched Mary's number of Cornholes, Peter steals Mary's 6 points. Peter now has 6 points to Mary's 12 points.

Paul: Throws one Cornhole. He has failed to match or exceed Peter's cornhole total. Therefore, Peter retains his 6 points and Paul receives none.

Going into round 3, Mary has 12, Peter 6 and Paul 0. Since Peter scored the most in round 2, he will pitch first in round 3, followed by Mary then Peter. This continues until someone reaches or exceeds 21 at the end of a round.

Cutthroat, Version 2

For this version you will need three sets of bags, each a different color. This is because all players start on the same side of the board and alternate throws until all 12 bags are thrown. As you might imagine, the scene can get pretty messy with the bags, depending on how many reach the board.

After all bags are thrown, the points are counted; 3 for a Cornhole and 1 for an Ace (see the Scoring section of this chapter) The player(s) with the lowest score receives zero points for that frame. The player(s) with the high score and second highest score, subtract the lowest score of that frame from their scored bags. The highest scoring player throws first in the next frame. He also chooses which side of the board to pitch from. The others must pitch from the opposite side. In a case where players are tied at frame's end with the highest score, honors default to whomever of those players pitched first in the last frame.

Here is an example of Round 1:

Snap: Throws two Cornholes and two on the board for a score of 8

Crackle: Throws one Cornhole and three on the board for a score of 6

Pop: Throws three Cornholes and one on the board for a score of 10

The lowest score is 6, posted by Crackle. He receives 0 points. Pop subtracts the lowest score, 6, from his score 10. Pop finishes with 4 points and Snap with 2 points. Pop is in the lead going into frame two, so he receives honors.

The first player to 21 (or exceeded) at the end of a frame's play, is the winner. In the case of a tie, those tied go into a sudden death frame(s) until a winner is determined.

Traveling King

This three-man game begins with two players at one board pitted against each other. The odd man out can be determined by coin toss, straws, arm-wrestling, whatever you deem appropriate. The first two competitors pitch a frame(s) until one scores using differential scoring (see the Scoring section of this chapter). This person becomes King and is honored. (see the

CORNHOLE RULES & REGULATIONS

Winning Honors section of this chapter). The King walks to his next opponent, the third-man out. These two pitch a frame. If the frame ends in a wash the King continues his travels, wash goes to the King. In order to dethrone the King, a player must beat him outright. This play is repeated until someone reaches (or exceeds) 21.

Here is an example of four frames:

Moe: Throws two Cornholes and two off the board for a score of 6

Larry: Throws one Cornhole and one Ace for a score of 4

Moe wins frame 1 with a cancellation score of 2. Larry receives 0 points. Moe is now known as Moe "the King" and travels to visit Curly's board on the other side.

Moe (King): Throws three Cornholes and one Ace for a score of 10

Curly: Throws four straight Cornholes for a score of 12

Curly garners 2 points and dethrones Moe for the crown. Moe keeps his two points, but will have to wait to add to his score. Curly now travels to the other side to face Larry.

Curly (King): Throws two Cornholes and two Aces for a score of 8

> Larry: Throws two Cornholes and two Aces as well, for a score of 8

This frame has ended in a wash. Therefore, Curly being the King, advances to pitch against Moe.

> Curly (King): Throws one Cornhole and three Aces for a score of 6
> Moe: Throws three Cornholes and one Ace for a score of 10

Moe has regained the title and 4 more points. He now has 6 points in total. This format continues until a permanent King reaches or exceeds 21.

Suicide Cornhole

The object of this 3-player Cornhole game is to have all your bags removed from play. Players alternate throws towards the same board. Using rally scoring, the player with the most points in a frame removes one of their bags from play. If two players are tied with high score, then all bags remain in play. Going into the next frame, the player with the most bags throws first and the one with the least throws last. When the bag amount is the same for two or more players, then throwing order is reversed from the previous frame.

Here is an example of one frame:

> Carson: Throws two Cornholes and two hit the ground for a score of 6.

Chad: Throws two Cornholes and one Ace for a score of 7.

Terrell: Throws one Cornhole and three Aces for a score of 6.

Chad has won frame one and therefore removes one of his bags from play. He now has only three bags to reach a high score. As you can see, it becomes increasingly difficult to remove your bags when others are at full strength.

Terrell goes first in frame two since he tied Carson, but went last the frame before. Carson follows and then Chad throws the first of his three bags. This process continues until one player has no more bags to sacrifice.

House Rule Variations

Presented below are two of the more common house rules that you may run into as you play Cornhole in different areas and/or with different people. Often you will find that certain house rules are played universally within a certain region. It is always a good idea to ask your host what house rules may apply to the Cornhole game. (see the Cornhole Skunk section of this chapter for a third commonly used house rule)

Setback scoring

Using this scoring system, a player must score exactly 21 to win the Cornhole game. Any score that goes over 21, sets the player back to a score of 13. Others play that the setback score is 15. Either way, you are penalized for not hitting 21 on the dot. This method can severely lengthen the game and is not recommended if others are waiting in the wings to play. This is particularly the case in a tournament environment. Furthermore, different strategies come into play. For instance, it may actually be in the best interest of the thrower to throw off the board in order for the math to position him at 21.

Two-pointer

Some boards come equipped with a one inch painted or taped ring around the hole. If you see this, there is a chance that your host plays for two-pointers. Any part of the bag that is touching this ring is considered two points. In the instance that a bag sits atop another bag and hangs over, but not on, the ring, then that bag also receives two points. In this case, the 'plane' of the ring is crossed and counts.

Win by Two

Sometimes the host will stipulate that a player or team must win by at least two. Therefore, if the score is 21 to 20, then the 21 is not a winner. Another frame(s) must be played until someone wins by two or more. In this case, the 20 has a shot to comeback and win the game.

Jack Bauer and Chuck Norris facts

Aside from being astounding Cornholers, these two warriors have other notable characteristics. Here are what I believe to be the top five most memorable for each.

Jack Bauer

5. If everyone listened to Jack Bauer, the show would be called 12.

4. If Jack Bauer was a Spartan in the movie 300, the movie would be called 1.

3. Vin Diesel can be rearranged to say "I end lives." Jack Bauer can be rearranged to say "Jack Bauer," which means the same thing.

2. If Jack Bauer was in a room with Hitler, Stalin, and Nina Meyers, and he had a gun with 2 bullets, he'd shoot Nina twice.

1. Jack Bauer once won a game of Connect 4 in 3 moves.

Chuck Norris

5. Chuck Norris sold his soul to the devil for his rugged good looks and unparalleled martial arts ability. Shortly after the transaction was finalized, Chuck roundhouse kicked the devil in the face and took his soul back. The devil, who appreciates irony, couldn't stay mad and admitted he should have seen it coming. They now play poker every second Wednesday of the month.

4. Chuck Norris does not hunt because the word hunting infers the probability of failure. Chuck Norris goes killing.

3. If you can see Chuck Norris, he can see you. If you can't see Chuck Norris you may be only seconds away from death.

2. A blind man once stepped on Chuck Norris' shoe. Chuck replied, "Don't you know who I am? I'm Chuck

Norris!" The mere mention of his name cured this man's blindness. Sadly the first, last, and only thing this man ever saw, was a fatal roundhouse delivered by Chuck Norris.

1. Chuck Norris' tears cure cancer. Too bad he has never cried.

RUNNING A CORNHOLE TOURNAMENT

"You know, the Oscar I was awarded for The Untouchables is a wonderful thing, but I can honestly say that I'd rather have won the U.S. Open Golf Tournament."

-Sean Connery

THE GAME OF CORNHOLE IS NOT ONLY A GAME for the family outing or friendly tailgate anymore. Cornhole has spread its wings to the tournament and league scene in recent years. No one knows about this progression more so than Michelle Cahill of NEO Cornhole. Michelle and her husband, Jim, formed the North East Ohio Cornhole, LLC in May of 2008. Their venture has led to one of the most respected and loved Cornhole league and tournament operations in the country. Michelle has graciously consulted on this chapter in an effort to spread the love of the game of Cornhole. Like many others she started playing Cornhole in the neighborhood before testing the tournament waters. Unlike many others, she made a giant leap, from tournament participant to tournament director.

This chapter will have advice for the tournament director who wishes to spread the game on a large scale or simply wants to throw together a day of Cornhole, beer and burgers amongst friends and family. Please note that the terms "player" and "team" are interchangeable depending if you are planning a singles or doubles tournament.

The Purpose

A tournament life cycle begins with a purpose or goal. If the primary driver of your Cornhole tournament is to produce individual profit, you may be in the wrong business. If this is your lone motivation, try a pyramid scheme or government bailout. Primarily, there are two good reasons to hold a Cornhole tournament; one to spread the love of the game and two, to raise funds for a charitable cause (or a combination of both). Take for example the last paragraph of the NEO Cornhole creed from their website - count how many times you see the word "love".

"We do this all out of a sheer love for the game. This is NOT a money maker for us, we just love doing it and we hope that you, the players love coming to our events and have a great time!"

A Cornhole tournament is an ideal way to bring together friends and families, in that anyone can play and requires very little cash to enter. As a director you can be responsible for providing this forum and as a result you will be raising Cornhole awareness in your area. You already know the lure of the game and how people react to it. Giving that gift to others is an added bonus to the Cornhole movement. As a tournament director, introducing players to the game will develop new talent and increase Cornhole participation.

Charity organizers are also becoming aware of Cornhole's allure. Many times a charitable organization will hold a Cornhole tournament to get people in the door. From there, profits from food, drink, raffles and other extras can rake in some solid dough. At the same time, these organizers may decide to pass around a mailing list to increase membership for their next event. A prime example of the Cornhole-charity relationship can be found in the Introduction of this book, where the American Cornhole Organization (ACO) and Easter Seals come together each year to help children and adults with disabilities attain greater independence.

Location, Location, Location

Your preparation before tournament play should start about one month before the event. The first thing you need to accomplish is deciding where the event will take place. Sometimes you will have a choice when it comes to location, other times the location will be given to you.

In either case, there are certain factors that need to be

meant on location before play can begin. The following is a checklist of questions that should be addressed:

- If played indoors, is there at least 12' of vertical height?
- Is there enough square footage for multiple boards?
- Indoors or parking lot?
- Will food and drink be made available?
- Are there adequate rest room accommodations?
- Do you need to acquire a permit for any outdoor affairs?

If you find a favorite bar that fits the bill, approach the bar owner with your idea. Keep your tournament date flexible for now, as the owner might want you to run your event during a traditionally slow day for his bar. After the weekend and Monday Night Football, Tuesday seems to be a popular slow day. Another common option is during the day of a Saturday or Sunday. This may work better if you plan the tournament to run long. Work with the bar owner for drink and appetizer deals for your players. If the bar isn't seeing much patronage normally at your proposed tournament date, then anybody you bring through the door is a bonus.

Sometimes, particularly in a tavern setting, food & drink and rest room accommodations will be met. In fact, the bar owner is counting on the increased revenue that your players will provide. This is one reason he has allowed you to use his venue. For charitable causes, usually the charity's director will provide food & drink as a way to collect funds for their cause. For those instances where you are left with no food & drink outlet, consider buying a bunch of pizzas or grilling out. Your average Cornholer will not expect a fancy catered event, but because tournaments can last long, it is important that you have prepared for fuel to be easily on hand. No surprise that beer is the most requested beverage. Make sure to have plenty of cold ones ready along with some bottled water. In the case you are providing food & drink, you can absorb the cost in the entry fee or charge a small price by item. Also consider the words "Free Beer" which may help the numbers game.

Promotion

A key ingredient to a tournament is people. You need players and your sponsoring bar expects more patrons. All your planning doesn't mean much unless you promote your event. Promotion starts immediately, preferably 30 days or more prior to the tournament. You will need to have a location and time determined, for your sales collateral. Here are some ideas to promote your tournament. Try to do them all, aside from calling Dolph Lundgren.

- Create an e-mail list and send a comprehensive message
- Participate in online message boards and Cornhole forums
- Place notices in church, school and city papers
- Display flyers and signs at local bars
- Display flyers and banners at location prior to event
- Local radio station plug
- Scout other Cornhole events for ideas
- Enlist a D-List actor to play in your tournament

In your correspondences, prioritize your message and fit as much onto the medium as possible. For instance, an e-mail can fit a lot of information, so put everything into your message, such as location, time, entry fee, prizes, format, charitable cause, rules and so on. You may have limited space for signs and flyers, so after the basics of location and time, display those ideas that will best attract your audience; "Free Beer", "Everyone plays 6 games minimum", "$1,500 Guaranteed Purse".

Keep your entry fees reasonable when promoting. Standard entry fees range from $20 - $40 per team. Suggest that your players pre-register, in an effort to get your tournament on their calendar immediately. Allow day of registration but at a slightly higher entry fee, as to encourage pre-registration.

Ineffective marketing implementation can sink your tournament before it starts. Be persistent and creative in your marketing efforts. You know your market, people and place, better than anyone, so don't limit yourself to only the bullet points listed above. Treat your tournament like a business and sell your concept anyway you can.

Sponsorship

A sponsor offers their sponsorship in the form of money and/or goods, in return for the opportunity to increase their brand image, which they hope will lead to support for their goods and services. If a sponsor does not believe consumers will react to their brand image, then the pursuit is fruitless, no matter how much advertising space you promise them. Your first goal, in finding sponsorship, is knowing your Cornhole market. Because you know who shows up to Cornhole events, you know what goods and services they use. For instance, since Cornhole is played in a social setting, beer vendors may be interested in sponsorship. You might not be able to get the big boys, Miller and Budweiser, but you may grab the attention of local breweries.

When your event is taking place, may affect who will offer sponsorship. The town's tax accountant may be willing to sponsor during tax season, or the firework stand might lay down a few hundred leading up to the Fourth of July.

Once you know who might be your target sponsors, approach them with your advertisement package. Seek multiple sponsors, and reward them based on how much money or goods they provide. A sponsorship package starts with your promotional materials. You can offer to place their logo and motto on all e-mails, banners, flyers and signs. Also, your equipment is a blank canvas for your sponsors branding. Decals can be put on the top and sides of boards. Think NASCAR, where the cars are plastered with branding, those displaying the largest images often pay the most. In fact, your sponsors may pick up the board costs if they get exclusive advertising on your boards. Your large scale bracket is another place for an all caps title of your sponsor. Your sponsor may also request a station where they can peddle their product. At Monster's Tailgate Bash in Fountain Square, the good people at Monster Energy handed out free samples and other doodads.

Make a list of all the possibilities where your sponsor may advertise and present that to them in your package. Know your real estate, in that, an image on your boards is worth more than a single sign on the wall.

Finding sponsors can help you offset the fixed costs of equipment and subsequent maintenance. Even more, sponsorship can increase your prize pool, which can increase participation. Sponsorship may ease the entry fee to your players or allow you to pay out more top finishers. If someone knows the top ten get paid, as opposed to the top three, they may be more willing to take their chances.

Keep diligent at finding new sponsors. Just like promotion to fill your bracket with players, treat your tournament like a business and sell your concept anyway you can when seeking sponsorship.

Bracketology

A good bracket is the foundation to smooth tournament play. Players and spectators will flock to your large scale bracket that charts the tournament progress. As a director you should take time in filling out an accurate bracket. A bracket that fails can have a snowball effect on the play of the tournament. Furthermore, when it comes to filling out a bracket, leave yourself some flexibility as to be prepared for more or fewer teams than you might expect.

"If the bracket is wrong, the entire event is wrong."

- Michelle Cahill, NEO Cornhole

Top Cornhole tournament directors recommend www.printyourbrackets.com for all your bracket needs. The site offers free and printable brackets that make a tournament director's job that much easier. The left-side menu on their homepage lists the various sport brackets presented. It is nice to see that Cornhole takes top billing. The following are the brackets available for use:

- Single Elimination Blind Draw, up to 64 teams
- Double Elimination Blind Draw, up to 36 teams
- Single Elimination Seeded, up to 64 teams
- Double Elimination Seeded, up to 21 teams

Remember to remain flexible with your brackets, as you may not know exactly how many teams will be showing up. If that is the case, make your best estimate. For example, if you think 15 teams will show up, print out the brackets for 10 teams through 20 teams. Even if you plan to use a computer, still bring printed copies on site in case your laptop should blue screen.

If you find your tournament participation flies through the roof and you burst through the ceiling of the brackets provided, you can still use the highest count bracket as a template to create your own.

Format

The format you choose will depend on the number of people participating, the talent level of the players and how much time you have dedicated to running the tournament play. The American Cornhole Association (ACA) recommends a double elimination seeded bracket format for tournament play. This means that teams are ranked and must lose twice before being eliminated from the tournament. [See Figure 4.0] Keep in mind that teams should face each other in a best of three series to determine a winner.

For smaller tournaments the ACA suggests that a round robin tournament is another viable option. A round robin format is a type of play where a player competes against everybody once. Round robin formats can also be found at www.printyourbrackets.com, along the top menu bar.

The round robin format can be pooled. This occurs when your tournament population is split into equal pool counts and everyone plays those within their pool once. For example, if 20 teams show up to your tournament, then you should make 4 pools of 5 teams a piece. PrintYourBrackets.com has templates for formats up to 18 teams per pool, but rarely will you have to go that high. Pools of 4 to 5 teams are ideal, if possible. See Figure 4.1 for a pool template consisting of 5 teams. If you have 20 teams, you will need to have four of these printed.

The optimal Cornhole tournament format is a combination of a round robin pools, followed by a double elimination bracket. There are a couple advantages of preempting a bracket with pool play. First, the talent level is exposed and allows for easier seeding. Second, and most important, every team will have played in four games before even starting the bracket. Participants want to get as much bang for their buck as

RUNNING A CORNHOLE TOURNAMENT

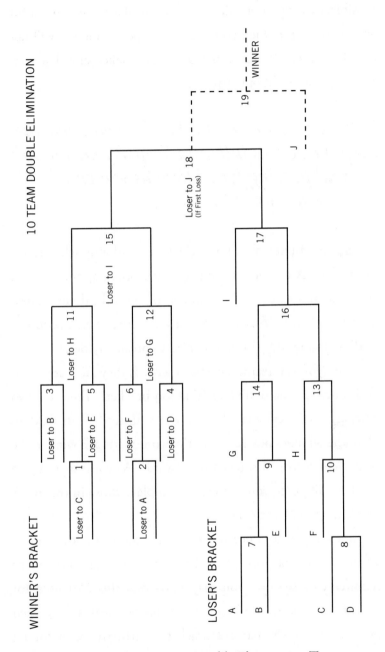

Figure 4.0: Cornhole 10 Team Double Elimination Tournament

possible. Your participation will sink if players only pitch for one or two games then go home. The sponsoring bar will not like this either. Round robin pool play makes sure that your players get their fill of Cornhole.

"The key is to not make the pools too big, keep the boards full, and keep as many people around playing for as long as you can."
- Michelle Cahill, NEO Cornhole

For the round robin pool selection, randomly select teams from a hat. After every team plays their pool opponents once, tally wins and scores to determine seeding for the double elimination bracket. Wins are normally the first consideration in seeding, followed by overall scoring to break any ties.

After your 20 teams have been seeded, they are ready to be positioned on the double elimination bracket. There are two brackets, a winner's and a loser's. Use your seeds, 1 thru 20, to fill in the winner's bracket first. Everyone starts as a winner, the equivalent to the "I showed up" award. As you progress, the bracket will guide you as to where to place those in the loser's bracket. [See Figure 4.1]

If timing is a concern, pool play can also allow you to advance only the top 12 or 16 teams, as your tournament requirements see fit. You may have seen this idea used for World Cup soccer, where only the top two teams from each pool make the tournament bracket. Furthermore, if timing remains a concern, a single-elimination bracket may be set-up

5 TEAM ROUND ROBIN

Team 1	Team 2	Team 3	Team 4	Team 5
W L	W L	W L	W L	W L

RND 1	RND 2	RND 3	RND 4	RND 5
1-4	3-1	5-3	2-5	4-2
2-3	4-5	1-2	3-4	5-1
5-Bye	2-Bye	4-Bye	1-Bye	3-Bye

Figure 4.1: Round Robin Tournament

after the round robin play. Some ACO events have a qualifier round followed by a single elimination tournament for their professional tour.

At all costs, a stand alone single-elimination tournament should be avoided. You will be hard pressed to collect an entry fee from anyone who might lose once and go home. Think golfing a round of nine holes. You have some bad holes and some good holes, and usually there is one shot you hit so perfectly that it keeps you coming back for more. Same is true for Cornhole. Anyone can have a bad game, but let them play as many as possible and chances are they will pitch that perfect frame or air-mail a beauty into the hole. You want Cornhole to be judged by that frame, not by one bad game. That frame is the hook that will keep your players coming back.

Addressing Skill Levels

Roughly ten years ago most Cornholers found themselves within the same skill range as their neighbor. Throwing four in the hole in one frame was an anomaly. Today, the elite player has been born and established. Where lines may have been fuzzy in the past, today's Cornhole has a clear set of professionals, amateurs and social players. Your tournament must address this shift in a practical manner. You don't want to scare away potential players who think they don't have a chance to win, and you don't want to stifle competitive play either.

There is no clear cut way to tackle this issue, but a number of ideas have been used with success. Use one of these concepts, or create a hybrid to fit your tournament requirements.

1. Do not allow professionals into your tournament
2. Create separate division brackets; competitive and social
3. Blind draw for teams
4. Split divisions after pool play

1. Professionals do not like this rule that much. Before eliminating a group of players, consider all other options.

2. Giving the choice of a competitive or social bracket can be especially appealing if you are hosting a benefit tournament. This way those who are showing up to support a cause can still enjoy some Cornhole action. If you create separate divisions, beware of "sandbaggers", who enter a division beneath their skill level to collect easy loot. These types also are also known

as "kittens". One way to deter this practice is to offer graduated payouts from competitive to social, so sandbagging doesn't get rewarded that much. For instance, the entry fee for the competitive division may be twice as much to enter, but the prize pool will be greater. As you run a few tournaments, identifying sandbaggers will become easier and you will be able to handle those situations personally.

3. Blind draws can lead to some interesting match-ups and provide a chance for everyone to get to know each other. A more refined blind draw is to have one hat with competitive players and the other with social players. From there, you select one player each from each hat and that forms a team. However, the con to this idea is that when money is on the line, competitive players do not respond well to being blindly matched with someone else.

4. If your format calls for a round robin pool play, a good idea is to use the final wins and scoring for each team to create a competitive and social bracket. If you have 20 teams, the top ten move forward and compete in a competitive bracket for more share of the prize pool. The bottom 10 enter a social bracket that still offers a reward, but not quite as much as the competitive bracket.

Equipment

You need top notch boards & bags and scoring scales to run a top notch tournament. Listen to your players about materiality. They will tell you what they expect. Refer to the guidelines from the Rules and Regulations chapter of this book for board & bag specifications.

In order to keep your tournament running at an acceptable pace, make sure you provide enough equipment to satisfy your tournament turn-out. As a rule-of-thumb try to follow the quarter theory. This theory states that you take your total team population and divide by 4 to arrive at the total number of board sets you need (two boards to a set). In practice, if you have 20 teams participating, you should have five sets of boards ready for play. This guarantees that at least half of your teams can be playing at one time and the other half can be running up a tab. This rule of thumb is fairly conservative, so don't worry if you fall a bit short or if your playing area will not fit that number of board sets. However, if you do have boards and space, consider putting out as many as feasible. Passers-by might want to test the game, or players might want to practice when they are not competing. The best sell of Cornhole is having someone play. If you notice a random person tossing bags on your extra boards, approach them and get their information for your next event.

A few days before your tournament launch, inspect all your equipment, boards and bags, for consistency and quality. Make replacements as necessary as your players will know the difference. Quality equipment will be a factor in their deciding to come back.

Day of Play

The day of the tournament can be an exciting time. All your planning and preparation will come to fruition. Before

RUNNING A CORNHOLE TOURNAMENT

heading to the location, check your packing list twice. In fact, it may be good practice to do this the night before for a tournament that starts early. Inevitably there is always one thing you might forget. Have help ready, who, at any moment, would be able to run an errand while you are hosting. Because you are the face of the tournament, try to stay on location.

You will want to make an announcement before the first bag is pitched. Aside from the standard "thank you and welcome" jargon, make sure to state the standard rules of play, and any "house" rules that may apply. See the Rule and Regulations chapter of this book. Your players will look to you to settle any disputes. Make sure you have a clear set of guidelines for your tournament and stick to them during the day of play. This applies to the format and payouts as well. Stick to and deliver what you promoted and promised to the players.

During play it is your responsibility to make sure the pace keeps steady. As a reference a 5-team pool can take about 1.5 to 2 hours to complete, followed by double elimination bracket which runs roughly another 1.5 to 2 hours. As tournament director, you need to play the role of "cattle herder", to make sure teams are where they are supposed to be in a timely manner.

A big problem during the day of the tournament may be player burn-out, in that, those players that get beat immediately have a sour taste in their mouth and will not come back. Pool play and double-elimination brackets should ease most of those concerns. Still, if you have the board space, considering running a separate "Toilet Bowl", to keep people playing.

This may take the form of a quick single-elimination bracket. Another idea is to have concurrent contests taking place such as a Cornhole long toss, where players pay a few bucks a throw to out-distance pitch others throughout the night. At the end of tournament play, you can announce the winner and distance of the long toss.

During the tournament you will form numerous friendly relationships. Everyone wants to meet the leader of an event. A lot of "Monday morning quarterbacks", will tell you how they would have handled certain portions of the tournament. Do not take these suggestions lightly or become defensive. Keeping the players happy will make your tournaments a success. Take on all advice and decide if a majority of your players would like to see implementation for your next tournament.

Paying-Out Cash and Prizes

Your participation turn-out will greatly effect your pay-outs. For your first tournament you may only have a rough estimate of the number of teams that will show up. Therefore, during promotion, the safest bet is to give a percentage-based pay-out structure. For instance, 50% to the winner, 25% to the runner-up and third place gets your entry fee back. Once you grow your participant list and have a historical footing you may be able to put actual dollar amounts on your prizes.

If you are able to get a sponsor with a cash prize, then your promotion will be that much easier. You can then guarantee a certain purse amount to attract players. Sponsors are also a good source for prizes such as hats, t-shirts and the like. The farther down you can award teams will help increase participation. If people feel they have a chance at coming away with some loot, then they are more prone to ante up. However, be careful not to dilute your cash purse too far down the final results, as to lose the value of competing. That scenario is simply a redistribution of wealth, and we all know that theory fails every time.

Single and ready to Mingle

Is there a better way to meet your soul-mate than at a Cornhole event? I can't think of one. Speed dating and outings for singles have become a popular trend. Your Cornhole tournament can take advantage of singles networking.

The optimal format is a blind draw for every round (round being three games) and participants cannot be paired with the same person twice. Be careful to sort girls in one hat and guys in another. The number of rounds is determined by how long you want the action to last or that your location allows. You must tally each individual's score for every round. For instance, say Tarzan, while teamed with Jane, scores 21-15, 23-16, 15-21 for a total cumulative point total of 59. He then is paired with Juliet where that duo scores a 55. Meanwhile, at another board Jane and Romeo have racked up 62 points. After two rounds, Tarzan would have 114 points, to Jane's 121.

In an effort to truly be corny, when the night ends, crown a King and Queen with a dinner for two at a romantic hideout.

A Cahill Introduction

"My husband and I are active, sports-loving people with a passion for competition. This passion led to our discovery of Cornhole. Our neighbors are avid Cornholers and you can always count on them pitching bags in their yard. One summer day, my neighbor threw down a challenge for a game of toss. My husband and I looked at each other, knowing full well we could not turn down this challenge. The game was played on plastic, flimsy boards like you might see at a tailgate party. The bags were floppy, and my neighbor just slapped the boards down with no concern for spacing. But none of this mattered. Even without standard equipment Cornhole can still be addictive. We didn't win the challenge on that day, but the game did provide the spark that led to our Cornhole addiction.

Shortly thereafter, we constructed our own boards and found a lady who made amazing bags. After two months of playing friendly games in our yard with the neighbors, we entered our first tournament. A nearby town was holding their annual "Homedays" celebration where the Cornhole tournament took place. My husband and I made a pretty good team, landing us in a second place finish. That experience sealed our fate. We were officially hooked to the game of Cornhole.

Several months would go by as we leisurely continued Cornholing and selling our friends on playing the game. Then one day we were enjoying some drinks at our local bar, talking Cornhole, when the owner asked if we might start a league at his establishment. We were excited to accept this challenge. The rest, as they say, is history. We formed that first league in May of 2008, and since then there hasn't been a Monday or Friday night (with various other nights here and there) that you can't find us both playing the awesome and addicting game of Cornhole.

Going forward we hope to build on our success, working with other organizations, to form a National Group of independent operators that offer nationwide league and tournament structure for all players at all skill levels."

- Michelle Cahill, NEO Cornhole

HOW TO PITCH IN THE HOLE

"You have to get your hands dirty first, before you can pull out your calculator."

 -Eugene Giorgio (my high school math teacher)

GENO RANDAZZO, OF MYCORNCOACH.COM, believes the perfect pitch is a beautiful thing to behold. He is considered the "Professor" of Cornhole, offering his advice in coaching others to pitch that perfect bag. The world's top two Cornholers, Matt Guy and Steve Vanderver, have also joined the MyCornCoach team. Together, they have a mission to bring the game to a whole new level, starting at the grass roots, in an effort to transform players into better Cornholers. Their video and board overlay come highly recommended.

I do not pretend to possess the perfect pitch. When watching the pros pitch I am immediately humbled. For this chapter I have leveraged the knowledge of many Cornhole professionals, particularly Geno.

Pitching Set-Up

Do you have a nephew who cleans up on the Cornhole boards at every family gathering? Do you figure it is time to turn the tables? When Cornhole first hit the scene, everyone played at a relatively equal standing. Today, as the game draws appeal, it has consequently drawn addicts; those who watch television and sleep with their bags. A hierarchy has formed in the Cornhole community. No longer can a lucky Cornhole here and a couple of bags on the board there, guarantee you the first to 21. While the professionals and amateur tournament players have displayed extraordinary Cornhole skills, the family grill-out games have also become increasingly competitive.

A player's journey of learning a game goes through three stages. The first being that the player becomes familiar with the rules and standards. Simply put, he knows how to show up and participant. He can keep score and knows when he is being cheated. The next stage involves refining his skills. For instance, playing Cornhole in the first stage, a player might try a few techniques to get the bag on the board or in the hole. His muscle memory has yet to kick in. By the second stage, a player feels comfortable in his throwing motion. During this stage, a player is extremely confident that he can, at the very least, get the bag on the board on every throw. The final stage is incorporating strategy within the confines of his new found talent. The strategy entails minding his environment and opponent.

This chapter will primarily focus on stage two - getting comfortable with an accurate pitching motion. The instruction is centered around the foundation and the toss. Within these two elements will follow specific instruction that will help you establish the fundamentals needed for accurate pitching. Make sure to master the fundamentals first, before adapting the pitch to your individual style.

The instruction will only be listed once, but should be repeated multiple times. How many repetitions? You will know the answer, when you stop consciously thinking about the instruction and just throw. This takes time and effort, and eventually the practice will pay dividends. Lucky for you, practice involves pitching, pitching and more pitching, something you love to do anyway; no running laps, no push-ups, no whistles. Just Cornhole.

"When I practice, I usually throw for a solid hour."

-Sheri Eggleton, ACO pro

Foundation and Positioning

I can still remember executing basketball drills on the gymnasium floor of St. Michael's grade school in Indiana. Size 8.5 shoes screeched as about ten of us shuffled left to right, back to forward, all in unison to our coach's direction. We were practicing our defensive stance and this was no fun at all.

Our awkward growing legs, perched bent at the knee, burned from the quads and the burn extended to the calves. Our arms reached out, stretching to cover an imaginary pass or shot. What a cruel way to start a practice. We would hit our first water break before even touching a ball. However, it was in those drilling moments of my budding athletic career, that I would learn that a solid foundational stance in sport is everything. Whether you are in the batter's box, awaiting a serve in volleyball, or lining up before the football is snapped, your foundation is the core to everything you accomplish next.

This is no different in Cornhole. The stance becomes magnified even more so when you consider the emphasis that pitching bags places on accuracy. Accuracy is not to be confused with precision, which is a degree of reproducibility. Reproducing the same throw off the board, while precise, is never a winning strategy. Instead your goal should be to accurately throw the bag in the hole with precision. The following stance will each give you the foundation to accomplish this.

"Think about it. The most accurate shot in basketball is a foul shot because there is less motion. You plant your feet, pick a foot to keep forward, bend your knees and sink it."
    -Mark Lambert, ACO Pro

The Single Threat
   In basketball, the triple threat stance allows you to pass, dribble or shoot, keeping your defensive opponent uneasy. In

CORNHOLE: THROWING BAGS IN A HOLE

Cornhole, the single threat allows you to do one thing; hole your bag.

1. Stand upright with your body and head pointed in the direction of the Cornhole board. Your head should stay level and eyes focused on the target during the throwing motion.
2. Widen your stance so that your feet are 3"-6" from shoulder width. This will give you stability during the toss.
3. Slightly bend at the knee, but be careful not to bend your back. A bent knee will help produce a more natural and smooth delivery, rather than a stiff stance that is rough on the body. Play compressed so you can stay low on the release.
4. Take one "walking step" forward with your weak foot. A right-handed thrower should step with his left foot.
5. Test the stance by moving your torso in a circle or having someone who likes you, give you a nudge. Your balance should hold.

"You want to dip the shoulder to the target you are releasing to; like you might in an egg or water balloon toss competition."
  -Geno Randazzo

The Power Step

For many, stepping into the throw, like you would a softball pitch, is natural and can be utilized in lieu of standing still. The number one Cornholer in the world, Matt Guy, uses a power step. No one style is best. Your comfort should be paramount when you are in the pitcher's box. Keep in mind that the same head and core tips above apply to the power step. The difference being that step four above, actually works in dynamic unison with the swing of your toss.

Throwing Flat

A bag the travels flat will be more consistent and easier to manipulate. A bag that breaks axis can be caught in the wind, land awkwardly or travel right off the board. By throwing flat you increase your chances that your bag will find the board and slide towards the hole in a controlled manner.

Throwing a flat bag starts with your grip on the bag. Most use either a wad, pinch or classic grip, and of those, the classic (or pancake or Frisbee) grip is the most popular. A wad grip is one where the hand scrunches the bag in an attempt to make a fist sandwich with a bag filling. The pinch grip is executed when the hand snips one corner of the bag in an effort to fling the bag towards the hole. If you want your bag to be unpredictable then by all means use the wad or pinch, but if you want to the throw a flat bag, the classic grip is the way to go. To grip classically, you want the contents of the bag to be evenly dispersed and balanced. The grip itself utilizes half the bag, where your thumb pushes down on the middle of the up side, and four fingers are tucked on the bottom side of the bag.

After grip, the release plays the final role in producing a flat bag. When you release the bag, your palm should open and face up, with your thumb almost reaching the high noon position. The finish should appear like you are trying to shake hands with the board. Do not pop your wrist, but instead rotate your forearm and wrist as one, at the time of the release.

The Toss Swing

Your toss swing should be relaxed and smooth, and oscillate like a pendulum. Every pendulum has a weight that is suspended from a pivot. In Cornhole, the bag is your weight and the ball & socket joint of your shoulder is the pivot. By its very nature, the shoulder's ball & socket joint allows you to have a free range of motion on multiple axes. This is in contrast to a pivot joint, such as the knee, where motion is in one direction. A robotic Cornhole player would have a pivot joint in the shoulder so as to act like a perfect pendulum. However, us humans, have free range in the shoulder and this freedom can actually hurt our toss. The pendulum is simple, so too should be your throwing motion. You never want to cross your body when tossing, leave that action to throwing a Frisbee. Nor do you want to bend your elbow, as that would add an unnecessary factor to the physics of the pendulum, something Galileo would not even want to address. A Cornhole toss more closely aligns with a softball or horseshoe pitch. Like these pitches, tossing a Cornhole bag stays within one vertical plane and does not cross horizontally. The closer you can have your shoulder's ball & socket joint act like a pivot joint, the better you will mimic a pendulum. This straight back and forth motion will result in better accuracy.

Rhythm

Rhythm is a movement to a timed sound or accent. Achieving a rhythm in Cornhole can be the difference between a win or loss. Time is invisible, finding it can prove difficult. Often, we place a beat or accent to a movement so we can measure time. Some examples are a ticking clock, dance steps or music. In Cornhole, you must find that measurement of time that works for you and repeat before each throw. Eventually your pre-toss, toss and follow through will be measured and appear like music to the eyes.

Practice your pre-throw routine, keeping the same timed movements. Adjust until your rhythm is comfortable with your style. Breathing techniques can help create a rhythm. One deep breath and a half exhale, can set your muscles and your timing. Visualizing is another technique to jump start your rhythm. Try looking at the board and visualize the flight of the bag and how you want the bag to travel. Once locked in, take a breath, step up and throw. However your pre-throw routine develops, make sure to keep it consistent. You will know when you have rhythm when you find yourself in the zone, so to speak. The zone is an athlete's happy place where there is little thinking, but instead just perfect reaction.

"Rhythm is important from the time the you pitch the first bag to the last. Losing rhythm can throw your entire toss off."
  -Sheri Eggleton, ACO pro

Perfect Practice

Practice alone does not make you a better Cornhole player, but perfect practice will. The types of practice you can undertake vary, because there are so many different types of boards, bags and course conditions. Try throwing on, with and in them all, both out and inside. Also, practice having your rhythm broken, and attempt to achieve it back. Scenario practicing is a popular way to improve your game. Recreate as many scenarios on the board as you can. Place blocker bags along the hole and practice pushing them in or going over the top of the blocker.

One method of practice involves goal setting. For example, promise yourself you won't stopping pitching bags, until you land at least two bags on the board in three consecutive frames. This method makes every pitch count and you will learn to focus on each throw. As you progress with your pitching create new goals for yourself. Maybe you don't stop throwing until you Cornhole two bags in two consecutive frames, or you score on twelve pitches in a row. If you find yourself accomplishing your goal after ten minutes, you need to adjust. Gauge your goals with your progress, always setting a goal slightly greater than the goal set the practice session before. Use this method, and before too long, you will find yourself chugging a beer, spinning around a dizzy bat and then sinking four consecutive Cornholes.

Watching Film

Every sense you can use to learn something should be utilized. Watching the top pros throw bags will give you a good visual to mimic. Try searching Google videos and YouTube to watch players like Matt Guy, Steve Vanderver and Randy Atha. Using the search words "King of Cornhole", will result in numerous videos of the King of Cornhole TV series, each episode lasting 20 minutes.

Imitation is the sincerest form of flattery. ACO professionals Mark Lambert and Dyana Tolliver, changed their tossing style to the no-step after observing Matt Guy using that technique in a video. Turns out they were watching the KOC TV series, where Guy implemented a no-step because the boards used for those tournaments were slick. Guy actually does use a power step in his throw. Still the duo found more accuracy and success imitating Guy's no-step throw and continue to use this technique today.

The "V" Shot

"V" is for Vanderver. Steve has one of the most unique styles of throwing known to mankind. Some call it a granny shot, I will describe it as the "V". Vanderver uses a stationary, staggered and wide stance. He cradles the bag in between his legs and then extends out and releases towards the target. When Eric Hinerman, ACO pro, first played with Steve on some practice boards before a match, Eric felt sorry for the guy. Eric would soon find out that the "V" is a deadly accurate shot that has launched Vanderver into a top two world position. Vanderver did not always use the "V". When first learning the game, he used a power step, but was consistently over-shooting the board. So he adapted a traditional stand-still shot, which resulted in much of the same. Finally, Steve mastered the "V" and has not looked back since. And others are taking notice, finding inspiration from Vanderver. Sean Short, ACO pro, has adopted the "V" as his throwing style of choice.

Figure 5.1: Matt Guy back swing

Figure 5.2: Matt Guy mid-swing

Figure 5.3: Matt Guy follow through

Figure 5.4: Steve Vanderver approach

Figure 5.5: Steve Vanderver mid-swing

CORNHOLE: THROWING BAGS IN A HOLE

Figure 5.6: Steve Vanderver follow through

Figure 5.7: Randy Atha- Toe, knee and elbow aligned

CORNHOLE: THROWING BAGS IN A HOLE

Figure 5.8: Geno Randazzo with Board Overlay

CORNHOLE STRATEGERY

"Oh, man. That was so much easier than putting. I should just try to get the ball in one shot every time."

-Happy Gilmore after hitting a hole-in-one

THE FINAL STAGE OF LEARNING A NEW GAME is incorporating strategy, after you have an understanding of the rules and a basic idea of technique. Strategy entails minding both environment and opponent. Your strategy is a game plan used to answer a number of "ifs". For instance, strategy will determine what you should do if a blocker is in front of the hole or if there are windy conditions. This chapter will touch on a number of "ifs" and possible strategies to incorporate for each.

While I have found some mild success pitching bags during my family's annual Tri-Lighter Classic, golf and corn fest, I am no pro. For this chapter I have leveraged the knowledge of

ACO professional Cornhole players who have logged numerous hours into the game. Strategy comes from experience. Whether through interview or direct quote, their strategy is filtered through me to you. Of particular guidance throughout this chapter was one Eric Hinerman, Manager of Agent Development for the ACO and a top ten professional.

Play Zone

Taking a look at a wide variety of bridges or just a peek at Epcot Center's "Spaceship Earth", and you should come to the conclusion that the triangle is the strongest of all shapes. The power of the triangle extends to the Cornhole board as well, more specifically an isosceles triangle. The hole being the top point of the triangle with two equidistant legs extending to the corners of the dead zone. This triangle is known as the play zone. [See Figure 6.0] Your Cornhole board may be a rectangle, but the only part of the board your bag should hit is the play zone triangle. The scrap areas of the board are known as the dead zone.

The bottom half of the play zone should only be used for sliders, as they start their board journey by hitting that half, but eventual rest in the hole or at the top half of the play zone.
The slide shot is the toss used most in a Cornhole player's arsenal. Keeping your slide distance minimal will keep errors to a minimum. However, when boards are slick, increasing slide distance is recommended.

Keeping your bag within the play zone forces you to stay in front of the hole. The risk of the airmail shot is that the bag

CORNHOLE STRATEGERY

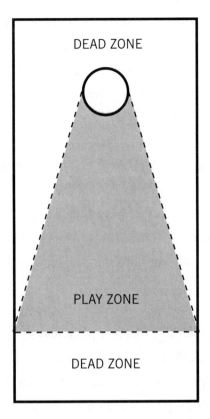

Figure 6.0: The Cornhole board play zone and dead zone

usually carries the play zone, and if it does not make the hole, then the bag goes long. Any bag in the dead zone is liable to be pushed out of play by your opponent.

Pitch Selection

Every Cornhole pitch counts. Think baseball, where a pitcher selects a specific pitch that is dependent on balls versus strikes, the hitter, the game situation, the weather and the lists go on. One of these factors or a combination thereof will determine if a pitcher throws a curve, two-seamer or straight heat and will also determine where, in or out of the strike zone, the pitcher would like the ball. The game's conditions have a similar effect in the game of Cornhole. There are three basic types of Cornhole tosses:

1. Slider - this bag hits board first before resting in the hole or close to the hole
2. Push-in - this bag pushes another bag into the hole or off the board
3. Airmail - this bag finds the hole without hitting the board

Constantly focusing on every pitch may seem daunting and tedious, particularly for a friendly outdoor game. However, the more you play, the more you learn about your opponent and the conditions, pitch selection can become almost second nature.

"For a big toss, take a deep breath and release half out, before throwing."
-Eric Hinerman, ACO pro

There are times, such as a tailgate or family outing, where the four bags provided to you for play are mismatches to each other. Two bags may be overstuffed, the third perfect for you and the last extremely flimsy. Do not randomly choose which bag to throw. Let the frame's action dictate which bag should be used. On every pitch, choose the bag that best accomplishes whatever result you need. A well-balanced bag may be suitable for an airmail shot, whereas a flimsy bag can be used as a defensive blocker.

The Coveted Airmail

An airmail occurs when a bag drops through the hole without touching or sliding up the board first. The airmail shot has become a necessary tool for any player's toss box. When competitive Cornhole began, playing conservative and waiting for an opponent's mistake would make for good strategy. Therefore, the airmail would not be needed. And still might not, depending on the competition level. But today the good players have an airmail shot to counter a good blocker defense.

To throw an airmail, simply straighten your posture or swing your arm faster. Never muscle an airmail shot. Some make the mistake of completely changing their style to create the extra distance needed. Your airmail should appear much like your normal slider shot, not much deviation is needed. The closer you can align the two, the greater your airmail percentage will climb. Another tip, for those using two-sided bags, is to throw your airmail on the sticky side. This accomplishes two things, first the bag will better grab any other of your bags looming around the hole and second, the airmail may stick to the back of the board if your shot goes long.

"Arm swing and tempo is very important to a properly placed bag."
-Mike Oehler, ACO pro

Until artificial intelligence is allowed in the Cornhole picture, throwing successful airmails will never be a guarantee. The biggest "D'oh" in Cornhole is the airmail gone array when a simple bag on the board would have done the job. While lethal, the airmail is the most overused shot in Cornhole. If your opponent throws first and lands a solid blocker near the hole, besides throwing a risky airmail to overcome his defense, try pushing his bag into the hole. You may find that your bag follows, or if it stops short, your opponent now has the decision to push-in or airmail. If he airmails and misses, you are set up perfectly for a push-in of your own bag. If he decides to push yours in, then that bag becomes as good as an airmail from you, without the risk. Clearing the board early in the frame is the best play. Pushing the bag in will put your opponent to the test. If you are not feeling the push-in shot, then another option is to stack your bag on his blocker. Again, the decision will be on your opponent to go for an airmail or throw yet another blocker. Try to force your opponent to throw as many airmails as possible. For your part, use the airmail at the end of a frame, and sparingly at that, when a score becomes a must and there is no other alternative. Before making that decision try moving in the pitcher's box to create an angle towards the hole. Sometimes an opponent's blocker only works when you are pitching straight on, but if you adjust your positioning, you may find his blocker no longer is a factor.

> *"If there is a bag in your direct line, sometimes you need to scoot over just a bit so you have a better slide shot to the hole."*
> -Sheri Eggleton, ACO pro

Weather Conditions

Natural forces beyond our control can dramatically dictate how Cornhole is played. Conditions such as humidity and wind each affect a bag toss a bit differently. A Cornhole player need know what certain conditions can do to a toss, and how to adjust accordingly.

Meteorology tells us that humidity is the amount of water vapor in the air. As humidity increases, Cornhole boards will become sticky. This is true indoors or out. A normal slide shot into the hole might fall short of the hole during a humid day. Water vapor in the air will decrease slide distance. One adjustment a Cornholer can make is to land his bag slightly up the board to compensate for the distance lost to humidity. Another method to ensure comparable slide distance is to add extra spin to your toss. A sticky board will have a harder time grabbing onto a bag that is spinning its way up towards the hole. Spin breaks the bag loose. With little to no spin a bag in humid weather will likely stick and flop. Next time you swing by the equator's Kuala Lumpur, have your spin ready, as they have nearly 80% humidity every day of the year. If your toss repertoire does not contain a good spin, try your luck in

Antarctica or the South Pole where humidity is at its lowest. When the water vapor in the air is low and conditions are dry, bag slide distance increases. If you are playing with a two sided bag, try using the sticky side for your slide shot to decrease your slide distance back to normal.

The biggest obstacle for Cornhole players is wind. The better players despise wind as it can be the great equalizer. A couple of practice throws can tell you how many inches a bag may sail from normal, and adjustments can be made from there. However, wind is not constant or predictable. The second you release the bag, the wind may decide to drop and the bag you overshot 6" to the left will embarrassingly miss the board. Traditionally, you are allotted 15 seconds to throw your bag so use that time to pick your moment. One method to ease the wind's power is to throw a lower arc shot while keeping your bag spinning flat. Most players release the bag around shoulder height, but in windy conditions, a waist high release point may be more suitable for a low arc. Leaning forward can also result in a similar low arc toss path.

Play Position

Throwing first is always an advantage as the lead bag determines how the frame will be played. A Cornhole from the start will put added pressure on your opponent to match. A blocker will leave your opponent with a decision to push-in or airmail. Take advantage of the lead bag every shot you get, so you can dictate the style of play. If you have thrown the lead bag in a given frame, and the frame's play gives you a choice of either throwing your last bag for points or for a wash, choose a wash. For instance, if a Cornhole will get you points, but an Ace will get you a wash, throw the Ace. Therefore, you are guaranteed lead bag in the next frame and can try to score at that time. If you get greedy and go for the points, and the higher risk airmail fails, your opponent may not only score, but he will grab lead bag back from you on the next frame.

Mental Game

Rhythm and momentum are crucial in Cornhole play. You want it and you want your opponent to lose it. If you notice that your opponent is a fast player, just itching to throw his next bag, then slow the game down. Remember, you have 15 seconds to pitch a bag. If your opponent has hit a rhythm and his momentum is scoring points on you, again, utilize your 15 seconds. This can be used much like a time-out is used in basketball by a coach who wants to break the opposing team's hot streak. Cornhole does allow a 30 second time-out per game. However, this is traditionally used as a chance to walk down to the board in play, in an effort to see how the bags lay. For instance, if two of your opponent's bags are one vibration away from the hole, then you may opt to throw off the board. Three simple words may also break your opponent's momentum, "watch your foot." Even if your opponent is legit with his foot, that seed of doubt will creep into his mind.

> *"If you walk slow enough to the boards, your opponent will pick up your bags for you."*
> -Randy Atha, ACO pro

If your rhythm is on fire and the momentum is going your way, stay focused and do not become lax. A big lead can disappear in a single frame of scoring. Once you get the best of your opponent, do not ease off, but instead finish them off.

> *"Step on the gas, foot on the throat."*
> -Matt Guy, ACO pro

DE - FENSE

In the game of Cornhole, a good defense scores points every time. In other games, a good defense may result in points. This can be seen in football when a cornerback intercepts the ball and runs in for a score or when a defensive lineman sacks the quarterback in the end zone for a safety. But in Cornhole, a good defense scores points every time. That was important to repeat, because it means that realistically you can win a game by playing only defense.

Shooting for the hole, you must hit a 6" diameter circle, which happens to cover an area of 28 inches squared. But playing defense you must only hit an area of 108 inches squared, almost four times the area of the hole. [See Figure 6.1] Granted, playing defense does take on less risk, thus less reward. However, your defensive bag offers three important advantages; scores one point, makes life for your opponent more difficult and your bag could be knocked into the hole for three points.

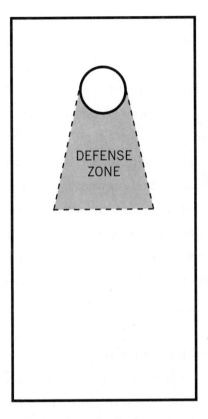

Figure 6.1: The Defense Zone

A good defensive throw goes for the hole, but if missed, is missed center and short. Attempting to throw a Cornhole, without focusing on a potential defense, may end with your bag past the hole on the board. A bag landing on the back of the board, while temporarily a score, is the worst position for a bag on the board. First, the bag is not blocking any potential Cornhole throw from your opponent. Furthermore, your opponent may be able to use the bag as a back stop or could knock your bag right off the board. Often times when your blood gets going and excitement is in the air, an overthrow occurs. If you sense that excitement, take a breath and cool your jets.

A good analogy comes from golf, specifically putting. A three-putt, after a killer drive and lay-up, can stick in the back of your mind for the rest of the round. Besides trying to nail the bottom of the cup, attempt to place the ball within an imaginary 10 foot diameter circle centered at the hole. This guarantees an easy 5 foot or less tap in, and everyone once in awhile you will sink that 30 foot putt. Same is true in Cornhole. Attempt to throw within the "108" area, and as you progress, more of your throws will find the hole. Practice so that if you're going to miss the hole, miss short.

Drinking Beers and Cornholing

In 1985 a Mr. Bill Smith won the World Series of Poker main event. The runner-up that year, T.J. Cloutier, described Smith as "the tightest player you'd ever played in your life when he was sober, the best player I'd ever played with when he was halfway drunk and the worst player I'd ever play when he got past that halfway mark."

Beer and Cornhole go together, that is a life truth. Beer will relax your muscles and may help with any tension before a big game. So having a couple beers will not hurt your game, until you pass your personal halfway mark. If you notice a little git-up in your gittalong, that might be a cue to ease off the bottle. From there some water or electrolyte rich drink should hydrate you back to normal.

Surviving

Sylvester Stallone, in preparation for Rocky III, attempted to obtain permission to use Queen's "Another One Bites the Dust." He failed. Undeterred, Stallone made a simple request of the band Survivor, to give him the most inspirational movie song of all time. They succeeded, with the release of "Eye of the Tiger" in 1982. If I had a forum to rank the six Rocky movies, I would go 4, 1, 2, 3, 6, 5. You can learn much about a man by his Rocky rating. But I digress.

How many times have you had a large lead on someone, say 16 to 2, only to have the game finish 21-16 in their favor? Or vice-versa. Momentum shifts within a match can occur frequently. The key is to survive your opponent's momentum.

In Rocky III the climatic fight pits Rocky against Clubber Lang, played by Mr. T or Laurence Tureaud to his family. In the first two rounds Clubber is throwing some hurt on Rocky, each punch is a knock-out one. Rocky stays on his feet, absorbing each hit. He survives.

Sometimes, when your opponent is air-mailing everything, you feel like your being knocked around. In these instances, stay calm and focus. Do not try to do something outside your capabilities. Trying too hard to match every Cornhole will throw off your delivery and possibly the bag from the board. Remember, Cornhole has a cancellation scoring system.

Sometimes the best strategy is to simply stop the bleeding.

When Rocky heads back to his corner at the end of round 2, his trainer, Apollo Creed, asks him what is going on in the ring. Rocky replies, "Its strategy, that's all, I know what I'm doing!" Rocky was taking the best punches Clubber had to offer and surviving. In round 3, Rocky taunts Clubber to hit harder, to punch faster. Eventually, Clubber loses his breathe and runs out of gas. Rocky smells blood and counters with a flurry of punches. The last, a vicious right windmill, catches Clubber and knocks him to the mat for a ten count.

No Cornholer is a robot, eventually a throw will miss the hole or the board all together. Be ready to strike when your opponent loses his momentum. Stay focused and consistent with your pitch. Your biggest mistake would be to alter your game and play his. Once the tide turns, do not let up. Always maintain the eye of the tiger.

Pardon me for a brief aside, but I cannot resist taking this time to throw out the top 3, Clubber Lang quotes from Rocky III.

3. "I reject the challenge 'cause Balboa is no challenge. But, I'd be more than happy to beat up on him some more."

2. Interviewer: "What's your prediction for the fight?"
   Clubber Lang: "My prediction?"
   Interviewer: "Yes, your prediction. "
   (Clubber peers into the camera)
   Clubber Lang: "Pain!"

1. "I pity the fool."

HOW TO BUILD A CORNHOLE BOARD

"The whole difference between construction and creation is exactly this: that a thing constructed can only be loved after it is constructed; but a thing created is loved before it exists."
    -Charles Dickens

CHANCES ARE IF YOU FLIPPED TO THIS CHAPTER, two things are true; you have already fallen in love with Cornhole and you happen to be a do-it-yourself type of guy. And so, this is just not a construction project for you, but a creation project, that will serve for timeless memories with friends and family.

However, if you are like me, all thumbs, then I have found some talented craftsmen who have honed the skill of board-making and bagmaking to an art. I recommend flipping to the Appendix and checking out some of the best manufacturers of boards and bags our country offers.

If you ever happen to bump into a boardmaker, you realize quickly how passionate they are about the process. This is their art and the board is their canvas. Most will customize the board to your needs whether its a design theme, graphics and colors, tabletop boards or boards that light in the night. There are all kinds.

When reviewing the materials needed, keep in mind your board will only be as good as the lumber you use. Take time to pick pieces of wood that are not split, chewed or warped. Look for the smoothest piece of plywood the lumber yard has to offer, ask an agent for the secret Cornhole stash if needed. The amount of effort you put into material choice will pay dividends later. Remember buying your wife's engagement ring, paying close attention to the Four C's, agonizing over Clarity, Carat, Cut, Color, before deciding on that one perfect diamond that expressed your undying love? Well, double that effort with your lumber choice.

Tools:
- Beer: 12-pack, even though this is a 4-beer job
- Clamps
- Compass
- Power Drill, with bits
- Protractor
- Sandpaper, medium grit
- Saw, Circular or Miter
- Saw, Jig or Band

- Tape Measure
- CornholeGamePlayers.com (use for building tips and answers to your questions)

Materials:
- Carriage Bolts: (4) 3/8" with wing nuts & washers
- Paint
- Plywood: (1) piece of 4' x 4' x 1/2", sanded.
- SPF Lumber: (4) pieces of 2"x 4" x 8'.
- Wood Filler
- Wood Screws: (1) box of 2-1/2"

STEP 1: Dimensions

Become familiar with the dimensions of a standard Cornhole board. While some boards are built to 36" in length, neither the American Cornhole Association (ACA), nor the American Cornhole Organization (ACO), recommends this length. [See Figure 7.1]

CORNHOLE: THROWING BAGS IN A HOLE

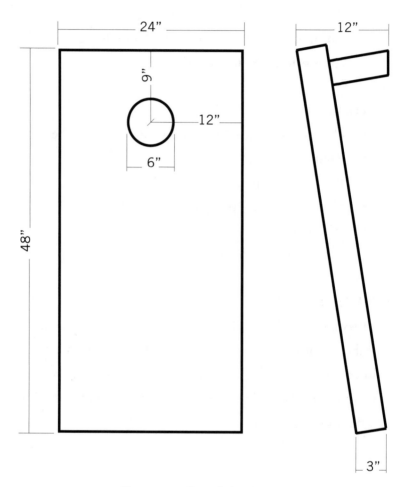

Figure 7.1: Board Dimensions

STEP 2: Cut your Wood

First you will cut the wood necessary for the board legs and frames. Take out your miter saw (or hand saw with miter box) and your four pieces of 2x4's. Cut the following quantity and lengths of 2x4's:

- (4) 48"
- (4) 21"
- (4) 11-5/8"

Tip 1: Do not forget to factor in the saw blade's width.
Tip 2: Do not make all your measurements at once. Measure then cut and repeat.

Now its time to cut some plywood. When purchased, one side of the plywood should already be 48" (good work). Pull out your circular or table saw, or use a hand saw as a last resort. Make a cut at 24" wide. Your 4' x 4' plywood sheet, is now two 4' x 2' board tops.

Tip 3: Have the lumber yard cut the plywood to size.

Take stock of your work, have some beer. You should have 14 pieces of wood ready for assembly.

STEP 3: The Frame

Grab your 48" and 21" cuts of 2x4's, along with the box of 2-1/2" wood screws. Pre-drill two holes from the 48" cut ends into the 21" cut ends, one on top and the other at the bottom. Screw in your screws at the pre-drilled holes. [See Figure 7.2] Repeat at the other side of the frame.

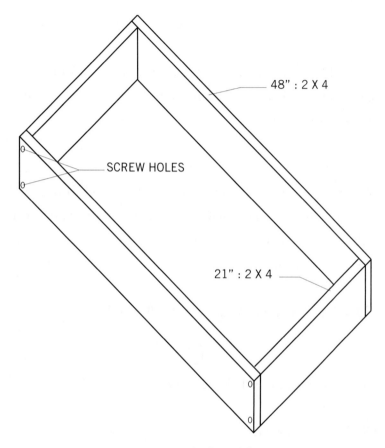

Figure 7.2: The board frame

Tip 4: When pre-drilling use a drill bit a tad smaller in diameter than the 2-1/2" wood screws.

Tip 5: Clamp the ends together when you drill and screw for a tight fit.

STEP 4: Attach the Plywood

Place the plywood surface on the frame. Pre-drill three holes along the top and bottom, evenly spaced from corner to middle to corner. Then pre-drill four more holes along the length of the board to the frame, two evenly spaced holes on each side. Screw in the 2-1/2" wood screws. [See Figure 7.3]

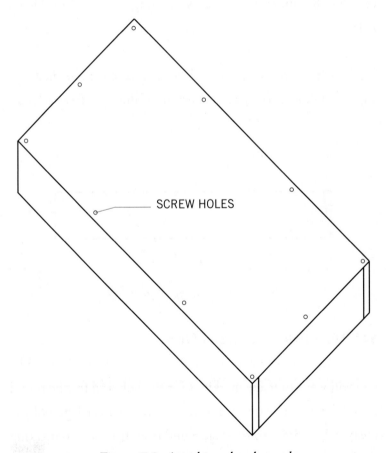

Figure 7.3: Attaching the plywood

Tip 6: Counter-sink the screws so that you can cover them with putty later.

STEP 5: Cut Angled Legs

Time to get your game face on, because dealing with the legs can be the toughest part of the board construction job. Take your 11-5/8" cut 2x4 and make a 81 degree cut, so that the 11-5/8" dimension remains the longest side. [See Figure 7.4]

Tip 7: Use a protractor to mark the angled cut to be made.
Tip 8: Double check the dimensions of the legs after each cut.

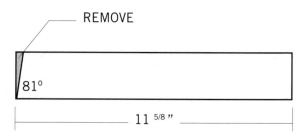

Figure 7.4: Cutting Angled Legs

STEP 6: Mark the Legs and Frame

At the opposite end of the 81 degree cut you just made, you will want to make markings for the bolt and for the round edge. Find the center point of the eventual carriage bolt by measuring 1-3/4" from the sides and from the top and marking the bisector of the two lines with a pencil. Next, pull out your compass. Use the center point to draw a half circle with a 1-3/4" radius. [See Figure 7.5]

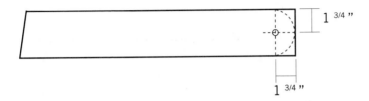

Figure 7.5: Marking the legs and frame

Next, mark the frame where the leg is to be inserted. You want to find the center point on the frame so that it matches the center point of the leg. Makes inserting the bolt easier. Again, you are looking for the bisector. Measure 3-1/4" from the top of the frame and draw a line. Measure 1-3/4" from the side of the frame that does not have the plywood attached. Where these two lines intersect is your center point of the frame. [See Figure 7.6]

Tip 9: Position the leg in the upper corner of the frame to get a feel of the center points aligning.

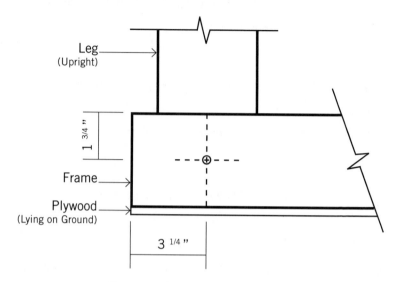

Figure 7.6: Center point of frame

STEP 7: Drilling the Legs and Frame

Clamp the leg onto the frame as it will eventually be attached as show in Figure 7.6. Drill a 3/8" hole through the table frame and corresponding leg at your bisected marks. The center points for each should be the drill target.

Tip 10: Use another 2x4 piece to sandwich the leg to allow for easier clamping.

Tip 11: With your leg temporarily clamped, stand the board up and make a sanity measurement.

STEP 8: Folding the Legs

You want the board legs to fold for easy transport to the tailgate. You have already made the half circle markings on the leg with you compass. Now pick up your miter or hand saw and make several rough cuts to achieve a rounded end. Next, take some sandpaper to the roughly rounded end and smooth. No need to overdo the sanding, as it will not be seen. But do smooth enough for the leg to be functional.

STEP 9: Assembly the Legs

Time to make it official and attach the leg to the frame. Gather your bolts, washers and wing nuts. Slip the carriage bolt into the frame hole and through the leg hole. Use a hammer to tap the carriage bolt shoulder into the wood so the bolt head becomes flush. Next, place the washer, followed by the wing nut on the leg side of the hole to hold the frame and leg together.

Tip 12: Test how the leg folds before fully tightening the washer and wing nut to the bolt.

STEP 10: The Hole

You will never throw a Cornhole until you cut the hole. This is the heart beat of the board and will give your board life. First, find the center of the hole, which is 9" from the top end of the board (top end being the end where you put your legs) and 12" from either side. Pull out your compass one more time and use the hole center point to draw a 6" diameter circle marking. Next, use your Big Papa drill bit to create a pilot hole. Use a jig saw and insert in the pilot hole to start your circular cut. Take your time with this cut. Finally, take some sandpaper to the hole edge to create a smooth finish.

Tip 13: If you have access to one, use a hole saw for an easier cut of the Cornhole.

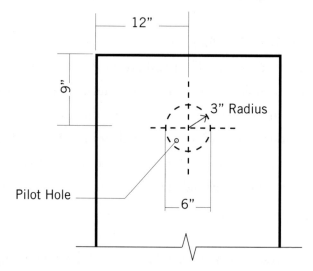

Figure 7.7: Cutting the hole

Painting

You now have a blank canvas in which you can apply a design. Painting is the traditional method to do so. Like with any good painting project half the battle is prepping your area. Make sure to putty wood filler into any screw holes or defects on the throwing plane of your board. Let the filler set. Use a medium grit sandpaper and smooth out the entire board plane as well as any bumps along the frame. After surface sanding, sand any sharp corners and edges, paying particular attention to the hole itself. Once your board is smooth ready, apply a primer to the entire face and let sit as instructed on the can. Finally, apply a semi-gloss or gloss latex paint to the throwing surface. Let dry then let the bags fly.

Check out this book's chapter on the Builder Community, for tips on how to let your creativity soar when designing your boards.

Plan B

If constructing is not quite your thing, there is another option. The tools you will need to execute plan B include:

- Beer: 12-pack
- Appendix 2.1 of this book
- Computer with Internet connection
- Credit Card

I am not going to proceed with instruction, but if you get stuck, at least you have twelve cold ones to keep you company.

The HOLE

If you happen to be by Milford, Ohio stop by "The Hole" retail shop, which sells boards & bags and other Cornhole accessories. The first of its kind, the store opened in October of 2007. The owner and operator is Frank Geers, President of the American Cornhole Organization.

BUILDER COMMUNITY

"An artist is a creature driven by demons. He doesn't know why they chose him and is usually too busy to wonder why."
   -*William Faulkner*

I READ ABOUT A GENTLEMAN who had been building boards for nine months before he pitched his first bag. Is it possible that some prefer the creation of boards more so than playing the game? After a brief perusal of the forum at CornholeGamePlayers.com and you will find that the answer is yes. The Cornhole Game Players website launched in March of 2006 under the direction of Jeremy Lindh. Today the site has nearly 2500 members, some of the top posters have names like Milky, TedNWV and derricksmash. Membership grew steadily, but in early '09 a different breed of member took over the site; the semi-professional board builder. Born was the forum of showing off board creations, discussing board business and extending helpful tips to others. The number and frequency of posts on the forum soared. While the site started as an area to discuss basic Cornhole game information, building and customization began to dominate, making Cornhole Game Players what it is today.

Community

The builder community is composed of the hobbyist and the professional, with various skill levels in between. No matter where a builder lands on the spectrum of boardmaking, the community has always been quick with a helping hand. Builders from different regions have actually referred business elsewhere to a save a customer shipping costs. A builder likes to talk shop and share lessons learned with novice builders. In fact, its a badge of honor to the community that a beginner can have success constructing a board on their first try.

The professional community is small enough where everyone has a pretty good idea of who's out there and what they are doing. It's not unusual for builders to meet up at Cornhole tournaments or even team up at an event. The Cornhole builders even have their own fantasy football league. And then there is the hobbyist who is not so well known. This builder advertises through word of mouth or maybe with lawn signs that read "Bean Bag Games for Sale." The vast majority of building is done at the hobbyist level.

Building is Contagious

Many in the builder community got hooked on boardmaking after making just one set for themselves. From that trial run, a friend, family member or neighbor took notice and asked if the builder wouldn't mind whipping a set up for them. Before too long this snowball's through an entire summer, resulting in quite a nice portfolio. For some that is a comfortable pace, building for family and friends, each time honing their skill and becoming more creative. For others, building continues on to a whole other level. The professional builder has made boardmaking a full blown business, equipped with branding and marketing tools online and outside the virtual.

A good indicator of where the game of Cornhole is treading can be seen by the builders popping up throughout the nation. While initially a Midwestern game, board builders are throwing the hammer in droves along the eastern seaboard and lately, building has taken off in California and Florida, as well.

Board Design

A Cornhole board maker is uniquely talented, in that, he must play the roles of carpenter and artist. Once the carpenter builds the framework the inner artist is presented with a blank canvas. There are many mediums to choose from such as paint, stain, decals, stencil, carving and burned branding. Once the applied tool is decided, a design must be executed.

From the beginning two types of designs have become the most prevalent, sport-themed and triangles, and in many cases a combination thereof. It makes sense that sport teams find their way on boards, given that Cornhole has been spread through the tailgate and marketed to the fanatic. The triangle design, starting from the hole and extending to the two bottom board corners, follows the recommended bag toss path. The triangle has become known as the Power Zone, and the corresponding design gives the Cornhole player a guide to the hole.

Lately, with Cornhole's growth to many different personalities, customization has become more prevalent. Board design has left its traditional comfort zone and delved into the realms of multiple themes such as music, microbreweries, cartoon, outer space, political, camouflage and people's tattoos. If you can dream it, someone can design it. The Cornhole board process has become so creative artistically, that the challenge feeds the builder's drive to build more.

The customization process takes time. It starts with a client idea that is fed to the builder. From there, the builder issues multiple mock-ups to the client for approval. This correspondence has been known to take weeks or even months, as the design becomes a very personal matter for client and builder. Once a design is determined, construction commences which can take days or weeks depending on complexity. I am reminded of the reality show, American Chopper, featuring Orange County Choppers where a camera crew follows the design and construction process of building a custom motorcycle. I wonder if the Discovery Channel or TLC would feature a Cornhole builder reality show.

The Future

The future for the boardmaker looks promising. However, boards are expensive to build, which means they're expensive to sell. This makes becoming a full-time boardmaker a difficult proposition. Full timers may help their cause by offering rental boards for tournaments and other like events. Still, instead, it is the part-time boardmaker that has found relative success in today's market. Most board retailers are constructing boards as their second job. As the game of Cornhole reaches out to untouched territories, and market exposure increases, the boardmaker will have a better shot at transitioning from part to full time.

Furthermore, as boardmaking becomes increasingly specialized, the average Joe may opt to hire a professional, besides taking a crack at building himself. The talent, art and creativity going into Cornhole boards are already making the craft difficult to imitate. Some are adding LED lighting to board edges and the hole for night time play. Gone are the days of the boxed and bulky Cornhole board with one coat of solid paint. Boards are becoming lighter, stronger and better suited for competitive play. Because of this progression, boards are not as easy to make as in years past. As boardmakers continue to hone their skill and increase efficiencies, they will widen the quality and quantity gap from the do-it-yourself guy. Once wide enough, the market trend for Cornhole boards will tip to the professional.

Consider that most players have no respect for smaller, inferior, plastic boards that are mass produced in Asia and sold at big box retailers. While costs to make and sell are cheaper, those serious about having fun with the game, more often than not, purchase a solid and well-constructed wooden board. The plastic imitations may work for kids or consumers who don't know any better. Cornhole is a unique case where the game actually loses it's appeal when the boards are mass produced. In the end, the true Cornhole board, as it is intended to be constructed, will be in most demand, and the professional boardmaker will be ready to supply.

A Builder's Story - Derrick Smash

I got my first look at a Cornhole board in 2003, at the University of Northern Illinois. A fellow Pi Kappa Alpha fraternity brother showed up one weekend with a set. I had never seen one before. He said, "these things are all over Minooka!" – Minooka, Illinois being his home town. At first, I ridiculed and mocked the game – but after reluctantly bearing through a few games, I was hooked. The game lay dormant in my life for a few years; playing it when it was around, once in a while playing in bar tournaments.

In April 2006, I found myself constrained to a wheelchair after a motorcycle wreck. I was stuck at home, and usually woke up every morning, 'gently' tossed my wheelchair off the front porch, hobbled down the stairs, and wheeled around to my garage to play with tools. Until this point in my life, I did not notice, but I had acquired quite a mechanic's tool collection from many years of working and messing around with cars. Seeing as I couldn't really crawl under a car for the time being, I busted out some tools that were sitting around and started working with wood. I built myself a workbench to accommodate the height of a wheelchair and just started to build stuff to kill time.

Come August, I was still confined to the wheelchair. I received an invitation to a wedding down in Springfield, Illinois. I figured making him a Cornhole set would be a pretty nifty idea. I got a buddy of mine to lug me over to the hardware store to buy a sheet of plywood and some dimensional lumber. A week or four later, I had completed two full sets – one for the bride & groom and one for myself. My friends and I brought both of them down to the wedding. I presented the bride & groom their present the following day at the brunch. They loved it, and one of their family members told me he would buy the other set. Sold. By February, I was out of the wheelchair and had already acquired several jigs and patterns made for mass production. Being in physical therapy 4 days a week definitely gave me enough time to play out in the shop. Over 1000 boards later, here I am, still customizing boards. And that's how it all began.

-Derrick "Smash" Pugh

CORNHOLE THE SPORT

"Anything we can all do can't be a sport...my mother can run, you don't see her on the cover of Sports Illustrated."

- George Carlin

THE AMERICAN CORNHOLE ORGANIZATION (ACO) is the governing body for the sport of Cornhole. Conceived in 2004 and incorporated in October of 2005, the ACO injects the game of Cornhole with a competitive spirit of well defined and branded professional and social tournaments in an effort to legitimize Cornhole's claim as a sport. The founder, Frank Geers set out on a mission to regulate the game, mold it and produce a marketable product to gain a spectator base for the professional class of Cornholers. His passion for shaping Cornhole into a sport is clear and can be seen by peeking at his pocket book; in order to finance the ACO he cashed out his

401(k) and took out a second mortgage on his house.

The ACO has roots at the epicenter of Cornhole's history, in Milford, Ohio, just 30 minutes from Cincinnati. Their presence can be felt across the nation, but particularly in the Midwest and sprinkled along the east coast. Currently, the organization's tournament directors can be found in Florida, Illinois, Indiana, Nevada, New Jersey, New York, North Carolina, Ohio, Oklahoma, South Carolina, Texas, Virginia, West Virginia and growing. The ACO tournament director has the privilege to hold sanctioned tournaments and leagues, following the rules and regulations the organization has set forth. The director also is considered a certified official, in that he can administer Social Skills Challenges. This challenge allows a player to rank himself so that he can compare his skill level to others across the nation. A player must play one Frame Game which consists of pitching four bags per frame for thirteen frames. The scores are accumulated, averaged by bags in the hole and bags on the board, and then sent to ACO headquarters for approval.

Depending on your score range, the ACO labels your level of play. I recently pitched a non-sanctioned frame game that puts me at a high-end "Backyard Holer", with aspirations on becoming a "Bag Bomber". To see how you might compare to the sport's best, view the latest rankings at www.americancornhole.org/rankings.

CORNHOLE THE SPORT

The following chapter will argue Cornhole as a sport and explore Cornhole's corresponding evolution in the sporting world. The chapter ends with a discussion on how best Cornhole may position itself to become part of the Olympics. Who better to consult on the topic of Cornhole sport, than Frank Geers, a major benefactor of Cornhole's sporting success. The ACO President has graciously offered his time and input throughout portions of this chapter, by quote and content.

Sport Defined

Webster's New World Dictionary, defines sport as "such an activity requiring vigorous bodily exertion and carried on, sometimes as a profession, according to some traditional form or set of rules, whether outdoors, as football, golf, etc., or indoors, as basketball, bowling, etc."

A Defense

Many are introduced to Cornhole at a tailgate or family outing. They are introduced to a game. Therefore, their default attitude to Cornhole will always be to view tossing bags in a hole as simply a game, no more. And that's okay, because Cornhole is a game that just so happens to also be a sport. The two co-exist, Cornhole the game and Cornhole the sport. This is the case for many activities. There is no sport involved when I bowl. When I throw between my legs or nail another gutter, I am in for fun, usually drinking beer and messing around with my buds. Rolling a 16-pounder down an alley becomes almost a secondary experience to the night. Contrast that with Norm

Duke bowling any one of his 58 perfect 300 games. What that man is doing is sport. Cornhole is no different, except that many haven't heard of or are just now becoming aware of professional Cornhole players, who consistently throw three of four bags in the hole, at least. To watch these professionals pitch bags is to believe that Cornhole can be a sport.

> *"The majority of the world can play the game, not everyone can play the sport."*
> - Frank Geers, ACO President

The professional Cornhole circuit is the product for the ACO. The professional Cornhole player has a history of competitive sport play, Eric Hinerman raced dirt bikes, Sheri Eggleton pitched softball and Mike Oehler bowled in college. Having a competitive spirit and athletic talent is a prerequisite for the professional. These players are decked in red, white and blue collared uniforms, with last names capped on their backs. The chest of the polo displays the ACO logo, a white silhouette of a man, bag just leaving his hand, on a blue and red backdrop. The colors and pattern purposely scream American tradition. Brand image goes a long way when wooing potential sponsors and giving credibility to the professional ranks within the sport of Cornhole. ESPN, the worldwide leader in sports, came out with an article, "Patchwork", that discusses the style and use of the American sports logo and common elements found throughout different sports. The article notes that the Jerry Dior designed MLB logo, inspired others, and goes on to list those sport organizations; National Basketball Association (NBA), National Football League (NFL), Indy Racing League (IRL) and included in the sport listing, our beloved Cornhole, under the ACO's logo.

Throwing a bag at a hole is easy, so is swinging a club at a white ball or shooting a ball at a basket. All sport stripped to its simplest form can seem easy, until you try to consistently hit the white ball on the green, hit a three-point shot or have the majority of your bags find the hole. The skill is the difference maker. A Cornhole player must possess a refined muscle memory, coupled with superb hand-eye coordination, along with a high level of mental toughness to complete, successfully, in a full days tournament. Muscle memory is a result of perfect practice. Not only must a pro throw endlessly, but he must throw the bag correctly. A professional may constantly refine their throwing motion depending on weather conditions and strategy. One cannot count on one static throwing motion for every throw. A professional must have a few toss types in their arsenal in order to combat an opponent's defense or environmental conditions. Mental toughness and endurance only make the physical aspect of the throw more strenuous. An average game for a player may go 20 frames or 80 bags per game per player. Most tournaments are played to a best of three format, and if they go to that third game a player will have thrown 240 bags to advance to the next match. Finally, to get through a field of 32, a player will throw in 5 matches for a total of 1200 thrown bags. Now consider that not only will throwing that number of bags get tiresome, but having every single one of those 1200 tosses matter could mentally drive a person nuts. Every bag counts, every toss has consequences. Bag 420 must be tossed with as much focus and strategy as bag 841. The day long focus alone meets sport's defined "vigorous" requirement. Combine that with blazing hot sun, strong winds and/or a competitor that is your equal, then professional Cornhole becomes something only a few driven individuals can accomplish.

> *"A critical attribute for the Cornhole player is the ability to focus, focus, focus."*
> - Frank Geers, ACO President

Steve Vanderver, a world top player (who, by the way, would buy the ACO if he won the lottery) breaks down a compelling argument using a comparison approach with basketball:

> *"The free throw shot is 13 feet to the front of the rim, 15 feet to the backboard, where you must throw a 12 inch ball into a 17 inch hoop. Furthermore, the three-point line is almost 24 feet away. Now look at Cornhole's hardest shot, the airmail, where you must throw a 6"x6" bag, 30 feet into a 6 inch diameter hole, precisely and accurately. The airmail shot and other precise shots that a Cornhole player has to make during a game, at the competitive level, is truly deserving of professional sport status."*

Sporting Evolution

The defined sport of Cornhole as we know it today is in a budding stage of laying the foundation for others to join the movement. Sports sociologists say one separation of game to sport is that sport's outcome has an importance to others outside those involved in the activity; or simply put, a fan base. The ACO is developing a group of personalities within the professional ranks that fans are starting to follow. In the beginning, primarily only players and their families had a vested interest in watching, but as the sport evolves and more become privy to the skill level displayed, more spectators have taken notice. The Tailgate Bash 2010 had streaming video of the final match, so that fans could watch Dale Smith knock off the world's number one player, Matt Guy. One way the ACO is drawing more fans is by strategically aligning events within activities that already have a built in audience such as NASCAR, NFL, MLB and college football games. Aside from their professional tour, the ACO is active in a grass roots movement to bring Cornhole the sport to colleges, high schools and middle schools in an effort to have children grow accustom to pitching bags. The kid picked last for the basketball team, may have a hidden talent for sinking a bag.

"Wherever there are competitive minded people, there is a place for Cornhole."
- Frank Geers, ACO President

The ACO has taken steps to promote the sport through its professional tour, materials and media. The tour is the first of its kind, where players are ranked by their Skill Challenge Rating or "SCR", which can be used as a handicap. The professional tour culminates in a King of Cornhole tournament once a year. The ACO was the first to televise Cornhole through their King of Cornhole television series. (Refer to "We are the Champions" chapter of this book for an in depth look at the KOC and its origins.) Another ACO media first was the creation of the Hole Magazine, found online at www.HoleMagazine.com. This periodical is strictly dedicated to the growth and celebration of Cornhole, both the sport and the game. Finally, the sport of Cornhole has taken advantage of two ACO bag innovations, the Players Choice bag and the resin filled bag. The Players Choice uses a different material on each flat surface of the bag. One side allows a bag to stick to the board, the other allows for easier sliding. In turn, this innovation created another layer of Cornhole strategy. The resin filled bag gives the professional Cornhole player consistency throughout all four of their bags and also happens to maintain better and last longer than traditional corn kernel stuffed bags. This is not much unlike the transformation of football material, that went from pigskin (actually pig bladder) to rubber, after scientist Charles Goodyear vulcanized rubber, allowing for stability and use in a wide variety of products.

A large part of the evolution of Cornhole sport is unwritten or better still, not even played. What we are witnessing today is what basketball might have been like in the 1940's, baseball at the turn of the 20th century, or the World Series of Poker in the 70's, when only a handful of buds sat down to play cards. As more people open their eyes to the sport of Cornhole, more will become addicted and drawn into the community.

"The ACO is similar to the giant bamboo that takes many years to develop a root system, and then grows 30" in a day. The ACO has been developing its root system for several years and the foundation of the sport of Cornhole has been laid. The growing years are now ahead for the ACO and Cornhole."
- Frank Geers, ACO President

Hall (and Hole) of Fame Induction

What do Cornholers Mark Lambert & Dyana Tolliver have in common with Jerry West, George Brett, Louis "Lou" Holtz and Randall "Randy" Moss? All these fine athletes have been inducted into the West Virginia Executive Sports Hall of Fame. The West Virginia Executive is the preeminent business publication for the state, who published a list of Hall of Famers in 2010. Each inductee is from the Mountain State, representing West Virginia with outstanding professional play in their given sport. This is the first time Cornhole has been recognized within an official sports hall of fame.

Lambert and Tolliver are both ACO professionals who consistently find themselves in the world's top 25 listing. Dyana Tolliver has achieved woman number one status. Mark

Lambert, an agent of the ACO, goes by Corn Dawg and is leader of the Cult of Cornhole with fellow professionals Steve Vanderver, Dale Smith, and Sheri Eggleton. These two Hall of Fame Mountaineers have also found success teaming up with each other in doubles tournaments.

The ACO has created a "Hole" of Fame, in Milford, Ohio, that is under construction, preparing for the inductions of Matt Guy and Chu Farsing.

Cornhole Olympic Consideration

There has been some talk around the boards that Cornhole should make a run as an Olympic sport. (And I'm not talking about the 2010 Senior Olympics in North Carolina where Cornhole made its debut among 90 participants.) Some may think the concept is pie in the sky, but others support the cause by using the "curling" argument. Curling is like shuffleboard, but on ice with brooms. This poor sport gets picked on quite a bit. The "curling" argument is simple, if curling is a sport than why not Cornhole. As Paul Nelson points out, other sports fall into the "curling" argument, such as ping pong, chess, ballroom dancing and korfball. Nelson is a producer, recently responsible for the documentary, "Brotherhood of Bags: Cornholing America." He also has initiated an online petition requesting that the International Olympic Committee (IOC) recognize Cornhole as an official Olympic sport.

Another Cornhole advocate for the Olympic push is ACO's President, Frank Geers. He believes that if ACO stays the course they could be the ones marching Cornhole into the

Olympics within the next 20 years.

Rio's Gain was Cornhole's Loss

The City of Chicago plastered the city with "Back the Bid" posters, murals, signage and other various reminders. The debate whether to host the games reached the television and radio waves. Concerned citizens cited historical economic data that appeared damaging to hosting cities post-Olympics. Others yearned for the chance to put Chicago on display to the rest of the world. A week before the announcement, Chicago brought the big guns to Copenhagen. It was here that the IOC would announce the city to host the 2016 Summer Olympics. Among the elite were Mayor Richard Daly, Oprah Winfrey and President Barack Obama. However, when the dust cleared, it was Rio, the first South American country to host, that won the bid. Chicago didn't even make it out of the first voting round. The city was in momentary shock. Even those who opposed the bid had to be surprised at Chicago's early exit.

What many in the Cornhole community didn't realize is that Chicago's failure, inadvertently, hurt any chance Cornhole had at making an Olympic admittance run. I doubt that was a concern of the President when he delivered his plea to the IOC. In fact, I further doubt the most powerful man in the world knows of the game Cornhole. One need only watch him throw a baseball on opening day to know that if he pitched a bag, it would look equally awkward.

The best chance Cornhole has to become recognized as an Olympic sport would be to petition for addition when the games are in the United States. We just missed with Chicago, but the next time a U.S.A. city hits the ballot, Cornholers from coast to coast should have a vested interest in the outcome.

We may have another chance come 2024, as there has been some talk that Philadelphia might put there hat in the ring for host city honors.

"We are the ones who will take the sport to the Olympics. This has always been a long term goal of the ACO."
 - Frank Geers, ACO President

Cornhole Recognition

The first step, for a sport to make the Olympic program, is to become recognized by the IOC. Recognition gets the sport into the consideration pool for inclusion. It does not guarantee the sport will be played in any given Olympics. For example, korfball, basketball for nerds, is recognized, but is not contested in the Olympics.

The IOC insists the sport is administered by an International Federation (IF), which ensures the sport's activities follow the Olympic charter. The IOC will look towards the IF to demonstrate that a sport meets certain criteria. The criteria are numerous and are included in seven major categories, 1) history & tradition, 2) popularity of the sport, 3) athletes health, 4) development of the IF, 5) universality, 6) image & environment and 7) costs. Before I take another joking jab at korfball, I should note their federation was founded in 1933.

Geers founded the American Cornhole Organization in 2004. That's not to say that Cornhole fans necessarily need to be patient because of this. In fact, before korfball had a federation, the game was a demonstration sport in the Olympic Games of 1920 and 1928.

As Cornhole stands today the game is primarily played in the United States, having recently spread its wings outside the Midwestern states. While our troops overseas have shared the game with the world, Cornhole has yet to catch worldwide fire. I selected three criteria from the popularity and universality categories. Currently the Cornhole federation would have a difficult time responding to some, if not all of these criteria:

- List of countries that have been placed in the top 16 in the last four world rankings.
- Number and list of countries that paid for TV rights to the World Championships held during the current Olympiad (the four years between Olympics).
- Number of national federations that organized national championships during the current Olympiad.

Some of these questions can seem overbearing, and they are, right now. Cornhole needs time to set a strong foundation in the sports arena, particularly worldwide, to be considered for recognition by the IOC. In order to accomplish this, the sport first must take care of business at home. Within the United States, Cornhole has the path of least resistance in becoming a recognized sport.

Demonstration Sport

Briefly touched on above, korfball was introduced to the Olympic games as a demonstration sport when the games were held in Antwerp, Belgium and again, eight years later, in Amsterdam, Netherlands. It is no coincidence that the sport thrives in those two countries. A demonstration sport is played during the Olympic Games in an effort to promote itself worldwide. No surprise that most demonstration sports get their start with the blessing and backing of the host country. This is why Cornhole must take advantage of any opportunity presented when America next goes to bid for the Olympics. To go full circle with the "curling" argument, this sport started as a demonstration one.

In 2008 the IOC allowed Beijing to run a concurrent Wushu Tournament along side the Olympics. Wushu, a form of Chinese martial arts, while not receiving demonstration sport status, did garner exposure.

The World Games

The World Games were introduced in 1981 as a substitute for games that did not make the Olympic cut. The triathlon and badminton events started in the World Games before becoming a part of the Olympics. Among the roughly 30 sports included are squash, water skiing, casting and body building.

A fair analogy would be this; the Olympics is to the NCAA Basketball Championship Tournament as the World Games is to the National Invitation Tournament (NIT). That is not to say Cornhole should snub its nose at the World Games, quite the opposite. Because the Olympics pose numerous hurdles, the first baby step for Cornhole may be to try to get included into the World Games. After all, these games are international and operate under the patronage of the International Olympic Committee (IOC). Cornhole would fall perfectly into the precision sport category which includes billiards, boules, bowling and archery. Bids for host city are currently taking place for 2017, and the Cornhole world should watch closely.

WE ARE THE CHAMPIONS

"Don't ever underestimate the heart of a champion!"
-Rudolph Tomjanovich, Houston Rockets coach.

CHAMPIONSHIP CORNHOLE HAS BECOME A REALITY over the last five years. Before this time it was difficult to narrow down the best in the world. The best was decided more by argument. This changed with the introduction of two popular Cornhole events, the King of Cornhole (KOC) and the World Championship of Cornhole. Both are annual tournaments. While the King of Cornhole has a mission to crown the single best Cornholer, the World Championship of Cornhole seeks to find the best Cornholing duo. (Both tournaments have singles and doubles events, but the premiere event for each tournament is noted as above.)

There is another interesting Championship beginning to

brew called the World Series of Bags (WSOB), expected to launch in July 2011. This tournament has qualifying events culminating in a final tournament at Chicago's Navy Pier. While a new entrant to Championship Cornhole, the WSOB does carry a lot of promise, as it has promoted a $50K first place prize to the winning team.

King of Cornhole

Do you remember a Mr. Jack Moran exclaiming, "That Smooooth Burger!"? If you followed WCPO-TV, channel 9 in Cincinnati, during the '60's, this piece of nostalgia might bring you back. Jack Moran, sports director of the station and former Cincinnati Reds announcer, hosted a show titled "King of TV Bowling". The show was sponsored by Burger Beer, a Cincinnati original. Every week Moran would televise a bowling tournament that culminated in that tourney's winner playing the reigning king.

The King of Cornhole was the brainchild of one Matt Gray who fondly remembers watching "King of TV Bowling", as a kid. After being introduced to the game, Gray reached out to his boss at WKRP-TV, requesting he consider using the "King of TV Bowling" format for Cornhole. The idea didn't fly. (If you are like me, you are now wondering "wasn't WKRP in Cincinnati a sitcom?" Well, as a matter of fact, it was. I suppose that makes Gray, Dr. Johnny Fever and his boss, Andy Travis.)

Matt Gray still thought his Cornhole program had promise. He reasoned that an audience would want to follow the best

Cornholers in the world throughout the year, rather than at just one event. Mustering some good old American entrepreneurial spirit, Gray used his own company, Gamemasters, and a little help from his friends, to purchase some airtime, in an effort to premiere the King of Cornhole. On July 7, 2006, Matt Gray's idea was launched. The show aired from Hippo Joes Bar & Grill in Cincinnati. The field started with 16 Cornholers, with the winner receiving $500 for his efforts. The production used a lot of purple backdrops, the color of royalty, when introducing competitors or cutting to different scenes. The lettering for the King of Cornhole was capped, bold and the color yellow. The sets of bags corresponded with this color pattern, one being purple, the other yellow. Cornhole partners Gil Flonkerton and Joe Fitzpatrick commentated the event, with interviewer Scott Yew, board-side.* The following table displays the final showdown participants and winner.

*Spoiler alert - The voices for Gil and Joe were played by KOC creator, Matt Gray and Phill Daniel, respectively. Scott Yew was played by Doug Hopkins.

You may remember Flonkerton from *The Office*, where the term was used as the national sport of Icelandic paper companies. Flonkerton translates to "Box of Paper Snowshoe Racing". The Flonkerton gold medal was awarded to Phyllis after she narrowly beat out Kevin.

KING	RUNNER-UP	DATE
Matt Guy	Theo Baca	07/07/06
Matt Guy	Chu Farfsing	07/14/06
Randy Atha	Matt Guy	07/21/06
Mike Bailey	Randy Atha	07/28/06
Randy Atha	Mike Bailey	08/04/06

KOC TV Week One

The first KOC pitted Matt Guy, representing Sneaky Pete's in the East Region versus Theo Baca, representing Deer Park Inn in the Central Region. Both players had similar styles, leaning into their toss with their right foot forward. Guy had defeated Mike Bailey pretty handily to make the final and rode that momentum into the match. For his part, Baca started off slow, grounding his first attempt. He picked it up however, matching Guy's four in the hole on two different occasions. However, simply keeping up with Guy did not help Baca's cause. Guy was relentless even when he was called for a foot foul. The game ended with a 21-0 score and handed Matt Guy the first KOC championship.

KOC TV Week Two

Guy defended his KOC championship the next week against challenger Chu Farfsing from Logos Sports Bar. This time around, Guy had very little warm-up, having only to play once the field of 16 gave him an opponent. The rust was evident, but of no real impact. Matt Guy dominated again, but this time the challenger was able to score. The final tally was 21-1.

On a side note, many professional Cornholers that pitch today recognize Chu Farsing as being instrumental in introducing the game of Cornhole to them. Farsing is described as a fun personality who cared more about spreading the love of the game, than his own competitive play.

KOC TV Week Three

For a second title defense, Matt Guy faced another challenger from Logos Sports Bar, this time Randy Atha. Very much like his first title defense, Guy showed some rust, but this time the impact was felt. Atha jumped to an early lead, 20-7, before Guy staged a comeback. Guy ripped off 9 unanswered points, but in the end Atha was too much. In the 24th cornrow, Guy hit the board high, leaving the hole exposed for an Atha Cornhole that sealed the deal. The match ended at 21-16. While Randy Atha did receive the $500, runner-up, this week, collected $200.

KOC TV Week Four

In week three of the KOC, Mike Bailey got crushed by Randy Atha, 21-0, in the tournament of 16. Going into week four, Bailey had hopes of redemption. But before meeting Atha in the final, Bailey had to defeat Matt Guy. Both players qualified through Century Inn, Guy having beaten Bailey during that qualifier. However, Bailey was rolling and took out Guy 21-12 for his chance at the King. During the pre-game interview, Atha displayed a purple crown, trimmed in white. There had been rumors of an elbow injury, but Atha assured everyone that he was 5 or 6 beers in and feeling good. Properly fueled, Atha jumped out to a 16-2 lead. But Bailey, would not go away, as he clawed his way back into the game. By cornrow 27, Bailey took the lead, 20-19. Atha had opportunities to close out the game in the late cornrows, but did not capitalize. Bailey grabbed the victory, 21-19, after 15 washes and 30 cornrows; both KOC records at the time.

KCO TV Week Five

Two familiar faces represented the KOC championship in week five. Randy Atha beat Matt Guy to get a chance to reclaim his title from the man who took it from him a week earlier in Mike Bailey. Much like the week prior, Atha pulled out to a big lead and by cornrow 12, he was up 16-4. Bailey's comeback reached double-digits, but went no further. Randy Atha won the game 21-10 to wear the crown one more time.

The KOC meets the ACO

The KOC TV series was only the beginning of bigger things to come. Matt Gray and his business partner, Doug Hopkins, had dreams of the "chase for the Crown." NASCAR races for the Sprint Cup and the PGA Tour swings for the Fedex Cup, so why couldn't Cornhole pitch for the Crown?

During one of the KOC qualifiers, Matt bumped into a Mr. Rick Taylor, who praised the work of the American Cornhole Organization (ACO). On Rick's urging, Matt and Doug agreed to meet with the ACO's president, Frank Geers.

As the meeting progressed, it became clear that visions between the KOC and ACO were aligned. Frank and the ACO were looking to expand their Cornhole events. The KOC had a winning formula for producing competitive play. In 2007, the two joined forces in an effort to forward the King of Cornhole concept, and Rick Taylor was recognized as the man who brought the ACO and the players together. The ACO had just named Matt Guy their National Champion in December of 2006*. Therefore, Guy received the King of Cornhole honor. A few changes were made, purple was out and now the KOC was branded pure gold. The following table displays the final showdown participants and winner, to date. It is not too hard to pinpoint the King for each year.

KING	RUNNER UP	VENUE	AREA	DATE
Matt Guy*	Theo Baca	Convention Center	Covington, KY	12/16/06
Matt Guy	Randy Atha	LV Sports Center	Las Vegas, NV	01/26/08
Matt Guy	Steve Vanderver	Sam Town's Casino	Las Vegas, NV	01/24/09
Matt Guy	Steve Vanderver	Orleans Casino	Las Vegas, NV	01/30/10

KOC 2007

For the first time the KOC moved its venue from the Midwest and headed for the bright light city of Las Vegas. The bags were tossed at the 93,000sf LV Sports Center.

During the KOC TV series, two men won the crown twice in the five weeks of competition. They met once in a championship match, with Randy Atha defeating Matt Guy. Since that game in 2006, Guy had been waiting to get a second chance at Atha for the crown. KOC 2007 gave him the opportunity. Guy came in ranked #1, to Atha's #5 ACO world ranking. He also came in confident knowing that if he played his game he could not be beat. Atha followed a simply strategy, "not to play stupid."

Unlike the TV broadcast, the championship match for the KOC 2007 was a best of three game series. Matt Guy had no problem taking the first game from a struggling Atha. And the second, for that matter, finishing the job 21-6 in defending his crown.

KOC 2008

Again the KOC shipped off to Vegas and this time pitched bags at Sam Town's Casino, one of Vegas' first local's casinos. Roughly 200 people traveled from across the nation to watch and play in the tournament. Aside from the KOC tournament, competitive doubles and social doubles were played on January 23 and 24. In fact, Matt Guy's younger son Shawn teamed up with Craig Tolliver to win the social doubles tournament.

Women Cornholers made some noise at this year's event. Four women qualified for the field of 64. Sheri Eggleton, an experienced horseshoe and softball pitcher from Indiana, and Dyana Tolliver of Ohio, both cracked into the sweet 16. Tolliver went on to win the competitive doubles tournament along with her partner Mark Allen.

The Vegas odds that someone named Guy would win the KOC increased, when Matt's son Bret squeaked into the final four. Bret's competitor was none only than his father. The student had yet to become the master. Matt took care of his son and #3 ranked Steve Vanderver took care of #2 Randy Atha to set-up the KOC final. While the competition level had climbed closer to Guy, the two-time champion completed the three-peat over Vanderver. The KOC 2008 kicked off a fierce rivalry between Guy and Vanderver, Cornhole's answer to the Jack Nicklaus / Arnold Palmer showdowns. The battle for number one continued through 2009 between Guy and Vanderver.

KOC 2009

Before Matt Guy could attempt his four-peat, he ran into a familiar foe in the semi-finals, Randy Atha. Guy took care of Atha in two games, beating him 21-12 in game two. However, the crowd favorite gave the audience a spectacular show in frame 15 before departing. With the board completely bag clean, Atha decided nonetheless to air-mail a Cornhole. The bag did not touch the board, all hole. The crowd gave a holler. After Guy slid a second one in, the board was again bag clean. This did not stop Atha from pitching another airmail with the same result. The crowd gave a hoot and holler. Guy's third bag fell short of the hole enough to be considered a blocker. I doubt it mattered that now Atha had a reason to attempt an airmail. Regardless of what Guy threw, everyone knew what was coming. And with another swish, Atha nailed a third airmailed Cornhole. The crowd was in a frenzy. Guy's final bag landed on the board. Everyone awaited Atha's final toss of the frame. Again, he pitched a high archer, that sailed through the sky, and fell down straight into the hole - four consecutive Cornholes that didn't touch the board. The crowd loved it and showed their appreciation. Atha was all smiles after the match, you would have thought he had won it all.

The championship showdown was a repeat of the year prior, Matt Guy versus Steve Vanderver. The match was split going into the deciding third game. Guy jumped out to an early 8-0 lead, until the 5th frame, when Vanderver hit an airmail that rewarded him his first point. By frame 8, Vanderver cut Guy's lead to half, 10-5, and had an opportunity to cut further in frame 9. Guy's first two bags missed the board long, but Vanderver could not capitalize. Guy holed his next two for a point and a 11-5 lead. Come frame 12, Vanderver holed all four of his bags and the score narrowed to 14-9. After Guy's airmail attempt knocked Vanderver's blocker into the hole, and his bag bounced off the board, the game became tense at 14-12. Vanderver rode this wave, air-mailing two in frame 15 for a 15-14 advantage. This was the first lead change of the game. The emcee took this time to announce to a cheering crowd that a new leader was in the building. In 16, Vanderver added two more. With the score at 17-14, Vanderver smelled victory and it showed when he took a moment mid-frame to check the score. Vanderver may have been too anxious for a win as a few of his bags flew long. Guy struck during this lapse with a huge 17th frame, taking back the lead 20-17. One point from victory in the 18th, Guy looked at a board with his own blocker in front of the hole. As his pitch sailed, a member of the audience screamed, "Two!". Sure enough the bag slid into his blocker and both found the bottom of the hole. Guy sealed his fourth straight King of Cornhole championship.

An emotional Guy hugged his bud and fellow Cornholer Geno and then his son Bret. The post-game interviewer asked, "Is there any other way to say 'wow'?" Guy's response, "yeah... tired, exhausted, worn-out." For his efforts, Guy was crowned, robed and given a check for $1,500.

World Championship of Cornhole

In the summer of '06, on a grassy field near a high school in the tiny village of South Webster, Ohio, the brainchild of founders Jack Williams and Rick Mays came to life. The World Championship of Cornhole was born. Their tournament started as a doubles competition, open to all players, from novice to expert. Round robin play that allowed for seeding into a bracket style tournament gave participants the most play for their buck. Today, the tournament has five championship events and most recently was played at a 9,000 seat arena.

From the onset, the World Championship tournament has been one for the players, and tournament director Jack Williams constantly looks for areas to implement improvements. In 2007, Jack understood the players needed quality boards & bags, so he partnered with Cornhole.com to provide the tournament equipment. That relationship still exists today and has grown into other mediums. In 2009, Jack and Rick introduced the Indiana Cornhole Girls. These ladies were such a hit, the next year they were brought back under the sponsorship of JP Ragon at Cornhole.com, and now have become known as the Cornhole.com girls. Jack continued to partner with others that shared his Cornhole passion. One match was with Geno Randazzo and the My Corn Coach team, who have an area designated for free mini-clinics to help players improve their Cornholing.

By 2010, the competition has grown to include players from 10 different states and one Canadian province. The team from Hagersville, Ontario, Nelson Cullen and his son Benjamin, traveled ten hours for the championship. For their efforts they were given the "Road Warrior" award. Even dignitaries are getting in on the Cornhole action. When the championship came to Huntington in 2010, Mayor Kim Wolfe threw out the ceremonial first pitch and holed it.

Participation has increased to roughly 300 Cornholers and the booty has risen as well. The purse, of $5,000, prorated by finish, goes into the pockets of the top 32 teams. Jack has found that the more people vying to be in the money the greater the interest in participation. With higher numbers and visibility, sponsorship has jumped on board. In 2009, Beef O'Brady's was the event's main sponsor and Miller Lite took that role in 2010. Also, in 2009, ESPN2 showed up to cover the main event, giving further exposure and legitimacy to the tournament.

The Cornholing now spans two days of pitching. The tournament series kicks off on a Saturday with the Juniors and Women championships. The day continues with the Tri-State Cornhole Championship where teams from West Virginia, Ohio and Kentucky compete for bragging rights. Saturday closes with the Downtown Throwdown, rewarding the best single's player in Cornhole. The main event of the weekend is held on Sunday, the World Championship of Cornhole. Below are selected results from the past couple years.

Champion Doubles Results

TEAM NAME	PLAYER 1	PLAYER 2	YEAR	CATEGORY
OK Connection	Matt Guy	Randy Atha	2009	World's
D&S	Dyana Tolliver	Sheri Eggleton	2009	Women's
Beef O'Boys	Bret Guy	Shawn Guy	2009	Junior's
OK Connection	Matt Guy	Randy Atha	2010	World's
Randazzo & George	Julie George	Margarita Randazzo	2010	Women's
Young Guns	Kyle Treedway	Derik Kins	2010	Junior's

We Are...Marshall

The first Campus Championship started as a partnership with Marshall University, the pride of Huntington, WV. The top two student teams from Marshall that advanced the furthest in the World Championship, then played each other for the coveted custom made wrestling-style belts. Introducing the local university to the Cornhole tournament mix has proven to be a popular method to spread competitive Cornhole to college students.

Tradition

Every championship event has a heavy dose of tradition, whether it be the Indy 500 winner chugging milk or the presentation of the green jacket at the Masters. Tradition enhances the culture of the event and the World Championship of Cornhole has started a couple.

The championship belts done with a pro-wrestling touch, have become synonymous with the event. Red, white and blue belts decorated with ornate gold embellishments, are given to the winners in the Junior's, Women's and Mixed divisions. The players describe the look as "unique" and "very cool", no doubt a popular item within the Cornhole culture. This type of gift has worked in the past, when the World Series of Poker gives a Neiman Marcus bracelet to the winner of their championship events, along with the cash prize. Every poker player wants a bracelet and every Cornholer wants a belt.

Each year Jack Williams holds a press conference to announce the host city for the next championship. This is much like the International Olympic Committee choosing and proclaiming the next Olympic host city. The decision itself carries weight, not just the actual play. This has turned out to be an effective way to get people hyped about the next championship. The decision also carries argument, as citizens from different towns plead their case.

Host City

CITY, STATE	DATE	LOCATION	EVENT #
South Webster, OH	2006	Field near high school	I
South Webster, OH	July 28, 2007	Field near high school	II
Portsmouth, OH	August 1-2, 2008	Second Street	III
Evansville, IN	September 5-6, 2009	Metro Sports Center	IV
Huntington, WV	September 4-5, 2010	Big Sandy Superstore Arena	V

CORNHOLE PLAYER BIOGRAPHIES

It's good to be king, if just for a while
To be there in velvet, yeah, to give 'em a smile
It's good to get high, and never come down
It's good to be king of your own little town
   - Tom Petty

BELOW I HAVE DOCUMENTED BRIEF BIOGRAPHIES on six of the most accomplished Cornholers in Cornhole's brief competitive history. Future Cornholers will be measured by the benchmarks these men and woman have set.

Matt Guy

Given Cornhole's position as a budding sporting revolution, Matt Guy can be considered the Ty Cobb of Cornhole, as he is the first player to dominate the sport. Before Cornhole, the National Horseshoe Pitchers Association of America ranked Guy as the sixth best horseshoe pitcher in the world. Today, in the Cornhole world, he is known simply as the King or Champ. Matt Guy has won the King of Cornhole for four years running and is the only king that tournament has known, as of 2009.

Matt Guy was born in Ft. Thomas, Kentucky and now lives with this wife and three sons in Alexandria, Kentucky. Currently, Guy works as a sales representative for Stigler Supply Company, a distributor in janitorial supplies and equipment. Though the longtime horseshoe player does have dreams that with Cornhole's explosion, larger purses may make a professional Cornhole salary, a sustainable one. His son, Bret, would also benefit from larger purses, as he has reached professional status under his father's tutelage.

In 2006, Guy joined the ACO circuit and went nearly four years without a loss on ACO boards. Though he had known about Cornhole since 1991, it would take 13 years before he realized his special talent for the game. This happened after winning a 2004 tournament at the US Bank Arena.

Selected Notable Finishes:
- First Place - Carson Palmer Cornhole Classic (This was the first ACO tournament he entered and for his efforts Guy received a camcorder.)
- First Place - King of Cornhole, 2006 thru 2009

Randy Atha

Above, I made the analogy that Guy was to Cornhole as Cobb was to baseball. Ty Cobb was a straight-laced fellow that completely dominated baseball in the early days. Toward the twilight of his career, another came to popularity with his beer drinking, good times, home runs and showmanship. That man was Babe Ruth. If you ask around, you will find that Randy "Hot Head" Atha has garnered that same adoration from the fans. Cobb hit for average, Ruth for power. A good story on how Atha entertains with power (airmailing Cornholes) can be found in the "We are the Champions" chapter of this book.

Born in Cornhole country, Cincinnati, and currently residing in God's country, Sharonville, Ohio, Randy Atha is married with one son, and works as a supervisor for Toyota Distribution. Atha recalls the early days of Cornhole when it was an anomaly to hit four Cornholes in one frame. One particular late evening at a public square, Atha and buds were pitching bags and knocking back brews, when the 5-0 came to investigate. The police overlooked any minor infractions, and instead joined in on the fun. Atha brings that same spirit of pitching with friends, to the competitions, and the fans love him for it.

Selected Notable Finishes:
- First Place - King of Cornhole TV Series, weeks 3 & 5
- Second Place - King of Cornhole, 2007

Chuck "Chu" Farsing (1954-2008)

One of Randy Atha's best friends was Chu Farsing, who had a deep love for the game of Cornhole and spread the game, with Atha, to local bars. Some of the bars that benefited from his appeal were Double D's, Sneaky Pete's, Century Inn and Logos Sports Bar. More importantly, Chu was the forerunner in introducing the game to many of the professional players today. His personality was contagious. Well known, many would spot him and scream "Hey Chu" to which he would respond "Bless You". Follow the laughs and fun and you would find Chu right in the middle.

Aside from Cornhole, he was also an avid softball player. On one occasion a player hit a towering home run over the fence, through Chu's car windshield and onto his front seat. Chu retrieved the ball, signed it and graciously presented it to the home run hitter.

Steve Vanderver

Steve Vanderver is the number two player in the world with ambition to take the top spot. He admits, until he takes down Matt Guy, he will not be satisfied. Vanderver shows a deep passion for the game and the growth of the sport. Born in Cincinnati, he currently calls Norwood, Ohio his home where he lives with his wife, daughter and son.

Vanderver has become known for his trademark tossing style, sometimes alluded to as the "granny" shot. Like so many others before him, Vanderver began pitching bags at tailgate parties and neighborhood grill outs. He started playing tournaments in 2004 and since has quickly racked up over 200 single and doubles victories. By 2007, Vanderver jumped onto the ACO professional circuit where his granny shot has become one of the most feared tosses in the game.

Selected Notable Finishes:
- First Place - Cornhole de Mayo, 2007
- Second Place - King of Cornhole, 2008 and 2009

Sheri Eggleton

Sheri Eggleton is from Indianapolis, Indiana where she works for the finance department of IUPUI, home of the Jaguars. Pitching has always been a talent of Sheri's, having played horseshoes and softball throughout her life.

Starting in 2005, Sheri added Cornhole to her pitching repertoire. She made a name for herself by nearly beating Randy Atha, the then #2 in the world, in an ACO TopGun event. In 2008 she broke into the sweet sixteen of the King of Cornhole tournament. The next year, she and Dyana Tolliver ran away with the women's World Championship of Cornhole and in 2010 Sheri became the first woman to seed in the Monster World Championships. A sport once dominated by men is starting to see women compete successfully at a world class level. Sheri is leading that charge.

Selected Notable Finishes:
- First Place - Boobs on the Move, doubles
- Second Place - ACO Spotlight Tournament

Dale Smith

Dale Smith from Campbellsville, Kentucky, has been hitting the boards every since discovering the game on the Fourth of July, 2007. Smith runs a family owned screen printing business. With his two boys grown, Dale is able to roam the tournament landscape. After meeting Steve Vanderver at a Knights of Columbus Cornhole event, the two traveled down to the Sunshine State, where they won two tournaments in one weekend. They have formed a solid doubles relationship since.

ACO Kentucky honored Dale Smith with the Most Outstanding Player of 2009 as a result of his play for the year in the Louisville area. His hot hand extended through 2010, having beat Matt Guy to become World Champion during the Easter Seal's Tailgate Bash in Cincinnati.

Selected Notable Finishes:

- First Place- Monster World Cornhole Championship, 2010
- Second Place - ACO WinterBlast, 2009

Jack Stagge

Jack Stagge has an obsession with Cornhole that keeps him throwing bags until dawn and has resulted in a world ranking of #3 in 2009. Born in Mariemont, Ohio and now living a touch further east in Lynchburg, Stagge is married with two daughters. Like many Cornholers, Jack, a southpaw, enjoys bowling and has many 300 games to his credit.

Set in Cincinnati's Fountain Square, the '09 World Championship is where Jack Stagge made a Cornhole splash. He defeated the #2 player in the world, Steve Vanderver in the final match to secure victory. But before tackling that obstacle, Stagge made history. Matt Guy had been untouchable for three years on ACO boards, until Stagge stepped up and knocked him down in the semi-finals.

Selected Notable Finishes:

- First Place - Monster World Cornhole Championship, 2009
- First Place - ACO Spartanburg, 2009

CORNHOLE: WHAT'S IN A NAME?

"And what's a cornhole tournament? Well, let's just say it's a cross between horse shoes and sodomy."
    -Stephen Colbert

Like the game, the name Cornhole is simple. Corn comes from the Proto-Germanic word kurnam, hypothetically speaking, in that Proto-Germanic is the hypothetical prehistoric ancestor of all Germanic languages. Comparable origins include korn, coren and kaurn, representing Old Saxon, Middle Dutch and Gothic, respectively. The word was understood by the locals to represent the leading crop of their district. In England, this meant wheat - oats in Scotland and Ireland, and rye in Germany. In America, maize, received the honored name of corn.

Hole also has roots in the Proto-Germanic tongue, coming from the word khulaz, meaning orifice or hollow place. The Germanic languages, English is an example, are opposite from the Romance languages spoken by the Italians, French and Spaniards. There is very little romance in the words "corn" and "hole". They are both four-letter, straightforward types, like their buddy "beer". Together these three provide for hours of fun.

The word Cornhole is a compound, the smashing of two old words to make a new word. More precisely a copulative compound, where A + B = the sum of the new word. This is in contrast to an endocentric compound where A + B describes a special kind of B, think beerbelly or houseboat. Cornhole is, instead, the sum of its parts. True to its linguistic form, the word ever so elegantly describes the game, functionally and strategically. Functionally, in that, a bag of corn and a board with a hole are used, and strategically, that the bag of corn is thrown into the hole. Strange how a game displayed so simply and played even simpler, can be extremely addicting.

This may have been a good stopping point for Cornhole etymology. I would prefer it was. My conclusion would have been; a simple word with a simple meaning for a simple game. Unfortunately, there is more to the word cornhole than meets the polite eye. I suppose, I could ignore it, but then the meaning would linger and grow. The best course of action in times like these is to admit and confront. So, please, let's dive in head first...

The Other Cornhole

Cornhole, anus; cornholing, anal sex. Laugh if you must, recoil in disgust if you choose, but when discussing the name of the game Cornhole, there is no hiding from this sophomoric unrelated slang. And so, I say, why not tackle this right away and move on.

Applying science, to almost anything, turns a childish chuckle into an intellectual yawn. Once something is analyzed to the minute detail, it ceases to have the same kick. Much like a magic trick with an exposed reveal. So let's do that, let's squash this unfortunate use of the term, so that the game Cornhole may own the true representation of it.

A Brief Termite Lesson

The termite, nature's answer to light-frame construction, can digest cellulose through its production of a cellulose enzyme, and with the help of symbiotic micro-organisms that live in the termite's guts. A termite relies on cellulose as a rich energy source to survive. Lucky for them, cellulose is the most common organic compound on Earth, comprising of 33% of all plant matter and 45% of wood content.

Two bullets to note from this termite discussion, one, that humans cannot produce a cellulose enzyme and two, the outer hull of corn is made of cellulose.

A Brief History of Man Lesson

A while back, say one million years ago, our ancestors were equipped with a longer digestive tract, able to handle the stresses of plant and vegetable matter. The diet of the Homo sapiens was primarily vegetarian in nature. Only recently during our stay on planet Earth have we adapted to a human society of carnivores, overtaking our primordial urge to gather roots and berries. Our digestion system adapted as well, to handle the rigors of the suburbia grill-out. With the digestion scales tipping towards meat, veggies have become more of a challenge to break down.

Also, courtesy of our new found diet, the Homo sapiens tooth structure has been altered. Dentition tells us that during the Flintstones era, we had larger molars able to mash and chew plant material. Today our meat diet depends on larger incisors, instead, to gnaw and tear our food.

Two bullets to note from this history of man lesson, one, that humans ability to digest corn has weakened and two, our teeth cannot mash corn like back in the day.

The Grill-Out

A smorgasbord of meats reaches the grill every summer weekend. A handful of veggies make the cut as well, and corn on the cob tops that list. A master griller, let's call him Gary, will soak the corn with husk in a bucket of sugar water. If Gary is feeling a bit saucy that particular afternoon, he will partially remove the husk and lather with butter, before wrapping back up. Once on the grill, the cob sits for a good forty-five minutes before being served.

Then the fun starts. Gary's guests shuck the husk and apply melted butter and salt to the kernels. Cobs are flying, bags are flying, as a dual game of Cornhole and corn eating is taking place. Gary and his guests are stuffed.

Inevitably, overeating leads to over-waste. Even Gary is feeling the hurt of the corn eating contest. Having eaten so quickly, he failed to chew the corn enough. But even if Gary had, his poorly evolved molars might not have been up to the task, his digestive tract sure wasn't. The tract was expecting some red-blooded meat. So Gary's grilled corn ends its journey partially surviving. Before the final flush, Gary takes a quick peek at the outer yellow hull of the kernel in his stool. The inside of the kernel, comprised of starch, sugar and oil was properly digested. The cellulose-heavy yellow hull stood its ground. Somewhat amused and confused by his trip to the bathroom, Gary, being also extremely clever, brainstorms how to relate the experience to his buds. Corn had survived right through his hole. Cornhole, voila. Gary shared his revelation of the term. His cohorts laughed. Thus, another cornhole was born.

Aside from leaves and paper, shelled cobs were burned for heat and stacked by outhouses as a rough substitute for toilet paper.

Cornhole Consequences

This unpleasant discovery on wordplay was enough for one of the industries bag & board producers to trademark Baggo, in an attempt to disassociate itself from the word cornhole. The company's disgust for the word cornhole is evident on their website, "...& was regionally known by many names, I.E. - polish horse shoes, Mexican bean bag toss, Corn hole... Ugh!"

The chief executive of Baggo Inc., Kirk Conville, argued that playing a game named cornhole is not appropriate for kids. Ironically enough, Baggo's preeminent purchaser is Dick's Sporting Goods. (Insert Beavis & Butthead chuckle.) And maybe someone should tell Mr. Conville that the word "bag" is not so innocent either; teabagging.

Still, the marketing effort to rid the world of the word cornhole, while futile, left a mark in some areas such as Chicago, where Cornhole is called Bags. This is a small consolation to Mr. Conville, who keeps a home in the posh Chicago suburb of Barrington.

Cornhole's Survival

The founders of the game had every intention to call it Cornhole. And why not? The game revolves around the simplicity of throwing a bag filled with corn into a hole. Cornhole. To change the name of the game would be imprudent. It would suggest that a tradition can be altered due to a transient sexual innuendo. Also consider that drawing opposition attention to the naming of Cornhole only empowers the negative connotation of the word. For example, imagine your child reading the Baggo website "Corn hole...Ugh!". Then coming to you and asking, "Why do they say ...Ugh!" Have fun with that conversation.

With the emergence of the American Cornhole Association (ACA), American Cornhole Organization (ACO) and the King of Cornhole, the name has set roots and should be celebrated, not shunned. No doubt the founders of the game were farmers, and probably extremely proud of their cash crop, corn. No need to strip that from the name because of a bunch of chuckling Buttheads.

CORNHOLE LINGO

"Jus' hang loose, blood. She gonna catch ya up on da' rebound on da' med side."
-Barbara Billingsley performing the jive scene from the movie "Airplane!".
(Also known for her role as June Cleaver)

A KEY INGREDIENT IN ESTABLISHING A UNIQUE CULTURE within a game comes from linguistics. The way that a society of people interact and communicate with each other, particularly through the spoken word, help define that group. Some words created by a game have become so woven into our vernacular that it is strange to think that at one time they were fresh and weird. Terms such as home run or touchdown come to mind. For example, the word touchdown comes from rugby, where a player must touch the ball to the ground when the ball enters the end zone. This is not a requirement for American football, yet the word has taken on its own meaning outside of its origination. To the game of football, the term has become synonymous with scoring 6 points. Terms, such as home run and touchdown, just scratch the surface of their respective games linguistics.

Eventually, if you want to become a part of the group, whether as participant or spectator, you must learn the lingo. The best way to enter the club is to jump in. The Cornhole community is a very welcoming crowd, no Ivy league requirements or rich dad needed.

The Cornhole society has begun the process of creating a special linguistic medium that allows us to best explain the happenings of the game. Once one surrounds themselves into a Cornhole environment, and throws a few pitches, the lingo and its meaning makes sense and becomes natural.

Because Cornhole, particularly competitive Cornhole, is in a budding stage, the game's jargon is continually growing. It is very likely that your group of family and friends, have created their own word descriptors that may catch on within the greater Cornhole society. Similarly, sects within the game, usually defined by locality, can use different jargon for the same situation. For instance, the Cincinnati Cornholer may call the game Cornhole, when someone in Chicago would call the game Bags. This difference is a good dynamic that only enhances Cornhole's culture with subcultures.

And so the following alphabetical list, while continually growing, is as complete as time has allowed.

Ace

An ace occurs when a bag lands on the board for a score of one point. Also known as a Cow Pie, Pimp or Woody.

Airmail

An airmail occurs when a bag drops through the hole without touching or sliding up the board first. Also known as a Swish.

Back Door

A back door occurs when a bag clears another bag that is blocking the hole and proceeds to enter the hole itself.

Backstop

A backstop is a bag that has found its way behind the hole, making it easier for the next pitcher to use that bag (backstop) as a way to bank his own bag into the hole.

Berlin Airlift

A Berlin Airlift is a throw used when your opponents bags are blocking the hole, much like a wall, and so you attempt to throw over that blocker wall.

> *"Mr. Gorbachev, tear down this wall!"*
> *-President Ronald Reagan in 1987 at the Brandenburg Gate.*
>
> (Feel free to shout out this one-liner after executing a 'Berlin Airlift'.)

Berlin Wall

A Berlin Wall is created when a thrower blocks the hole with a wall of his bags.

Blocker

A blocker is an Ace in front of the hole that makes it virtually impossible for a Slider to reach the hole unless the Slider puts both bags in the hole. A well-positioned blocker also hinders an arc toss and bounce into the hole. The only throw immune from a blocker is an Airmail throw. Also known as a Pimp.

Blockn'

Blockn' is the act and execution of a Blocker. Blockn' is used as a defensive maneuver, particularly versus a player who prefers to slide the bag into the hole.

Candy Corn

Candy corn describes a throw that results in the bag not reaching the front of the board. The expression applies weakness from the thrower. Also known as Corn patty or Sally.

Chances Double

The chances double expression is called out after your opponent throws a Cornhole, in the hopes that your next throw matches the challenge. The hope is rooted in a form of gambler's fallacy.

Cincinnati Slide

The Cincinnati slide occurs when you throw your bag hard and without much loft so that it knocks your previously thrown bag into the hole. Also known as a Driver.

Cornfusion

Confusion is a state of being when two players or two teams cannot agree of the score after an inning of throws.

Cornhole

Cornhole is the result of throwing your bag into the hole, which scores 3 points. Also known as a Drain "O".

Cornholer

Cornholer is a person who plays the game Cornhole, often times to the point of obsession.

Corn-nuts

Corn-nuts is a frustrated throw intentionally missing the board and instead aimed at your opponents mid-region.

Corn Patty

See Candy corn.

Cow Pie

See Ace.

Damage Control

Damage control is a strategy used to cancel as many of your opponent's points after they have tossed numerous Cornholes.

Dirty Bag

A dirty bag is a bag that hits the ground before reaching the board or is on both the board and ground. Also known as a Grounder or Short bag.

Double Deuce

A double deuce is accomplished when you throw four Cornholes in one inning without the help of your opponent. Also known as a Four-bagger, Galbraith, Gusher or Slam.

Drain "O"

See Cornhole.

Driver

See Cincinnati Slide.

Faultin'

See Foot Fault.

Foot Fault

A foot fault is an infraction when you step past the front edge of the board during your toss.

Frat House

Frat house describes a board where all four of your bags and all four of your opponent's have landed. The inning is a wash and no one score any points. Also known as a Power Wash.

Frisbee

See Pancake.

Frontin'

See Foot Fault.

Four-bagger

See Double Deuce.

Galbraith

See Double Deuce. Can be expressed in fractions such as a quarter Galbraith, half Galbraith, and three quarter Galbraith.

Grounder

See Dirty Bag.

Gusher

See Double Deuce.

Hanger

A hangar describes an Ace on the lip of the hole, in a position to drop. Also known as a Lipper or Shook.

Honors

Honors is the privilege to throw first and is awarded to the player that was the last to score in an inning.

Hooker

A hooker is a bag that is thrown so after it hits the board it curves around your opponents blocker and into the hole.

Jumper

A jumper is a bag that bounces off a previously thrown Ace and then continues its journey by going into the hole.

Leprechaun

A leprechaun occurs when you throw all four bags on the board (four Aces) without getting any into the hole (no Cornholes).

Lick Side

The lick side is the right side throwing position for a right-handed player, and the left side for a left-handed player.

Lipper

See Hangar.

No Blood

No blood refers to an inning where no one scores.

Pancake

A pancake describes a bag's flight motion as one that doesn't flip end over end, instead the the surface of the bag remains parallel with the ground. Also known as Frisbee or UFO.

Pimp

See Blocker.

Police

The police is the Cornhole referee of a game.

Power Wash

See Frat House.

Push Bag

A push bag pushes 2, or more, previously thrown bags into the hole.

Put it in the basement

Put it in the basement is an expression that refers to your partners request to throw a Cornhole.

Rolly Polly

A rolly polly occurs when a tossed bag rolls over a Blocker and into the hole.

Sally

See Candy corn.

Shooter

The shooter is the person who is tossing the bag.

Short Bag

See Dirty Bag.

Shucker

A shucker occurs when a bag is thrown, striking your opponent's bag off the board.

Shutout

See Skunk.

Skunk

A skunk is a game that ends in 7-0, 11-0 or 13-0, depending at what rules you follow. Also known as a Shutout or Whitewash.

Slam

See Double Deuce.

Slick Woody

A slick woody is a bag that slides into the hole. Also known as a Slick Willie.

Slick Willie

See Slick Woody.

Slider

See Slick Woody.

Splitter

A splitter is a bag toss that is thrown with enough force to split two of your opponent's Blockers and land in the hole. Also known as Splitting the Red Sea.

Splitting the Red Sea

See Splitter.

> *Let my people go!"*
> -Charlton Heston playing Moses.
> (Feel free to shout out this one-liner after 'Splitting the Red Sea'.)

Stanker

A stanker is a thrown bag that does not land on the board or in the hole, resulting in zero points for that throw.

Stiff Bag

A stiff bag is one thrown poorly as a result of competitive pressure.

Swish

See Airmail.

Taint

A taint is a bag that lands anywhere between the front of the board and the hole.

UFO

See Pancake.

Wash

A wash occurs when an inning's score is zero for each player or team.

Whitewash

See Skunk.

Woody

See Ace.

ACKNOWLEDGEMENTS

I AM HONORED TO HAVE BEEN WELCOMED into the Cornhole community during such a pivotal time in the game's growth. This has easily been the most enjoyable writing experience I have ever had, and I owe that in large part to a slew of Cornholers. Frank Geers, Eric Hinerman and the entire ACO family have been more than accommodating with any request. Within my sweet home Chicago, Geno Randazzo's enthusiasm for Cornhole is inspiring. I don't know of anyone who loves the game more than Michelle Cahill, and I thank her for that. Jeremy Lindh and Derrick Pugh opened my eyes to a completely other subculture of Cornhole, the builders. And Michael Whitton is a constant reminder of how Cornhole brings people together. I look forward to growing these relationships as Cornhole grows.

I would be remiss if I did not recognize those behind the scenes. The talented team at my publisher, Amalgam Studio, were instrumental in breathing life into the pages of this book. My editor in life, my mother, Susan, took time to edit every word I threw at her. A big hug to my wife, Lisa, for her patience and understanding during my pursuit of Cornhole literature.

APPENDIX

Builder Information

A good builder will listen to your needs and exceed your expectations. Here are some Cornhole builders, to check out, that have met that grade.

American Cornhole
http://www.americancornhole.com
1-888-563-2002
sales@americancornhole.com

AJJ Cornhole
"Your One Stop Cornhole Shop"
http://www.ajjcornhole.com
1-888-504-7112

Cornhole.com
http://www.cornhole.com
1-877-672-6769
play@cornhole.com

Derrick Smash
http://www.derricksmash.com
773-968-2863
info@derricksmash.com

Indy Custom Cornhole
http://www.indycustomcornhole.com
317-339-0780
Contact@IndyCustomCornhole.com

Mountain State Cornhole
http://www.mountainstatecornhole.com
wvcornhole@suddenlink.net

NapervilleBags, Inc.
"A Custom Cornhole Company"
Sales, Rentals, and Tournaments
http://www.napervillebags.com
630-885-7872
Chris@NapervilleBags.com

Victory Tailgate
http://www.victorytailgate.com
407-704-8775

INDEX

People of Cornhole

Allen, Mark	163
Atha, Randy	97, 105, 116, 159, 160, 161, 162, 163, 164, 165, 168, 173, 174, 176
Baca, Theo	159, 162
Bailey, Mike	159, 160, 161
Cahill, Jim	67
Cahill, Michelle	67, 74, 78, 87, 198
Conteduca, Rocky	37
Daniel, Phill	158
Eggleton, Sheri	90, 96, 136, 144, 150, 163, 168, 176
Farsing, Chuck "Chu"	150, 160, 174
Flonkerton, Guy	158
Fitzpatrick, Joe	158
Geers, Frank	36, 38, 133, 141, 143, 144, 146, 147, 149, 150, 152, 153, 161, 198
George, Julie	168
Gray, Matt	157, 158, 161
Guy, Bret	163, 166, 168, 172

Guy, Matt	88, 93, 97, 99, 100, 101, 116, 147, 150, 159, 160, 161, 162, 163, 164, 165, 168, 172, 175, 177, 178
Guy, Shawn	168
Hinerman, Eric	98, 108, 110, 144, 198
Hopkins, Doug	158, 161
Lambert, Mark	91, 97, 149, 150
Lindh, Jeremy	134, 198
Mays, Rick	166
Nelson, Paul	150
Oehler, Mike	112, 144
Pugh, Derrick "Smash"	134, 139, 140, 198, 200
Ragon, JP	166
Randazzo, Geno	88, 89, 92, 106, 166, 167, 198
Randazzo, Margarita	168
Short, Sean	98
Smith, Dale	147, 150, 177
Stagge, Jack	178
Taylor, Rick	161, 162
Tolliver, Craig	163
Tolliver, Dyana	97, 149, 163, 168, 176
Vanderver, Steve	36, 88, 97, 98, 102, 103, 104, 146, 150, 162, 164, 165, 175, 177, 178
Whitton, Mike	6, 7, 41, 47, 198
Williams, Jack	166, 169
Yew, Scott	158